UNEQUAL OPPORTUNITY: A CRISIS IN AMERICA'S SCHOOLS?

Bruce M. Mitchell
Robert E. Salsbury

BERGIN & GARVEY
Westport, Connecticut • London

Library of Congress Cataloging-in-Publication Data

Mitchell, Bruce M.
    Unequal opportunity : a crisis in America's schools? / Bruce M. Mitchell and Robert
E. Salsbury.
        p.   cm
    Includes bibliographical references and index.
    ISBN 0–89789–720–X (alk. paper)
        1. Educational equalization—United States.   2. Discrimination in education—
United States.   3. Socially handicapped children—Education—United States.   I.
Salsbury, Robert E.   II. Title.
LC213.2 .M58   2002
379.2'6'0973—dc21   2001037913

British Library Cataloguing in Publication Data is available.

Library of Congress Catalog Card Number: 2001037913
ISBN: 0–89789–720–X

First published in 2002

Bergin & Garvey, 88 Post Road West, Westport, CT 06881
An imprint of Greenwood Publishing Group, Inc.
www.greenwood.com

Printed in the United States of America

The paper used in this book complies with the
Permanent Paper Standard issued by the National
Information Standards Organization (Z39.48–1984).

10 9 8 7 6 5 4 3 2 1

Contents

Preface

During the last three decades of the 20th century, the authors have conducted research, taught classes, and written books and articles about multicultural education. We have examined the issues of educational equity, racism, sexism, and the historical exploitation of the poverty powerless who often have been the innocent victim of callous socioeconomic exploitation.

Obviously, these issues have had dramatic effects on the nation's school children because all schools around the world reflect the values of the society in which they find themselves. While the authors have argued that America's pluralism may be its most important natural resource, it is obvious that this cultural/racial/ethnic/religious diversity has also caused nearly insurmountable problems throughout the land.

Even today racism still plagues U.S. citizens who are not European Americans. For example, Michael Wilson of the *Washington Post* described a discouraging reaction to baseball pitcher, John Rocker's unfortunate comments in an April 23, 2000 article which appeared in the *Seattle Times*. Rocker, who was suspended for his remarks against virtually any American who was not from a European American background, has been given standing ovations in Atlanta and other cities. Wilson argued that Rocker's comments may have reflected the reactions of many Americans. Moreover, his remarks were similar to those made daily by some right-wing radio talk show hosts all over the land.

Sadly, racism in the United States seems to be making a comeback, necessitating increased efforts on the part of classroom teachers to help their students acquire more positive attitudes about our nation's diverse populations. Hence, it would appear that the need for multicultural education programs in the schools still needs to be included in curricular offerings. These racist attitudes have been around for years, and they are learned from parents at a very early age. Unfortunately, they are often quite deeply entrenched and difficult to dispel. But in order to understand how all this fits in, it is necessary to examine the historical roots of American education and the macroculture in which it has flourished.

After the American Revolution, it became necessary to make key decisions about the type of education which should exist in the new nation. Since the topic of education was not addressed in the country's constitution, that function was left up to the individual states, which sometimes created problems related to their economic status. States, such as Massachusetts, developed strong systems of public education in keeping with Thomas Jefferson's notion of the need for a strong public education system but others were much slower to follow suit.

As a general rule, Native Americans were not involved in formal education in the early days. Nearly all the tribes were illiterate since they lived clear across the Atlantic from Gutenberg, Germany, where the printing press was invented. Slavery prevented many African Americans from becoming literate because of the prohibitive practices and actual laws which made it difficult to acquire such skills until well after the termination of the Civil War. Moreover, throughout the history of the country, adequate schools sometimes were not readily available for the children of cheap laborers. Consequently, a patchwork quilt of education was unfolding in the absence of central direction. Some children had ready access to excellent public and private schools while others did not.

Due to the constitutional requirement of church and state separation, religion has been legally banned from the public school curriculum for much of the nation's history. And while children have always been free to pray by themselves, formally led prayer by educators has been judged to be unconstitutional in the public schools. Some of this interpretation of the U.S. Constitution can be traced back to Thomas Jefferson's notion of the "wall of separation" between church and state. Because of the secularization of the nation's public school system, new private religious schools have surfaced lately in increasing numbers, partly for the purpose of including religious dogma in the curriculum. During the latter few decades, public schools have suffered from declining test scores and increased levels of violence. Zero-tolerance restrictions are now common in many parts of the country because of the easy availability of guns and other weapons. The supposed decline in public education has caused more and more parents to leave the public schools. Consequently, increases in private school enrollments and a burgeoning interest in home schooling have had a profound effect on public schools.

But let's return to the question of unequal opportunity in America's schools. Is the inequality approaching crisis proportions in a country which constitutionally guarantees equal opportunities? Or was the Fourteenth Amendment's Equal Protection clause merely a fanciful idea which had no possibility of becoming fulfilled?

An underlying problem may be even more profound. Private schools require tuition payments and many parents can't afford to leave the public schools.

According to some critics, since private schools tend to be populated by affluent European American children, they may have acquired an elitist flavor. Could that mean that the public school system in the United States might become a "pauper system?"

Jefferson's argument for a strong public education system meant that in order to make our constitutionally driven form of government function properly, ALL children are entitled to a public education regardless of race, gender, ethnicity, national origin, or handicaps, etc. Moreover, all children are entitled to equal educational opportunities by virtue of Fourteenth Amendment edicts.

Thus, the purpose of this book is threefold, we wished to examine the issues of equality as they affect the schools. If equality of opportunity is denied, what damage might it cause? And most important, how can public school parents get the best possible education for their children without opting for private schools or home schooling?

We designed the work to be of interest to the general public and parents alike. By addressing the complicated issues of human diversity in the United States, we feel the book will be useful for serious students of multicultural education. The need for such continuing school efforts can be seen from the reference to the *Washington Post/Seattle Times* article mentioned earlier.

And the words of John Dewey will be first and foremost in our minds as we address these topics. In his classic work, *Democracy and Education*, he wrote: "What the best and wisest parent wants for his own child, that must the community want for its children. Any other idea for our schools is narrow and unlovely; acted upon, it destroys our democracy."

Introduction

As the United States enters the next millennium, it seems appropriate to examine the general health of the nation's system of public education which has served the Republic so well during its post-revolutionary history. However, that system is under enormous attack at the present time, and it is even conceivable that drastic changes could be in order during the early stages of the 21st century. All of the 50 states have articulated new and lofty educational goals for the year 2000. Thus, numerous changes in education can be anticipated.

Arguments for a strong system of public education were made during the post-Columbian period of American history. Perhaps the overriding issue was that the oppression encountered in Europe should be avoided at all costs. Thus, many principles of egalitarianism were incorporated into the very creation of the U.S. Constitution. However, the subsequent translations have presented enormous challenges for the various U.S. Supreme Courts due to the politicization of those bodies.

Horace Mann, Henry Barnard, and James Carter were three of the early influential educators who vigorously championed the cause of free public education for all American children. The result was that gradually, the notion of a strong, free system of public education for all American children regardless of race, gender, religion, or socioeconomic status began to evolve. However, this idea was not fully accepted and it often took landmark Supreme Court decisions, such as *Brown v. Board of Education* before the concept of educational equality would spread to some parts of the country.

Unfortunately, during the last half of the 20th century, public schools in America have been under attack. Influential critics such as Admiral H. Rickover and author William Bennett, former secretary of education, have been quite vocal in their criticisms of public education in the United States. However, other critics, such as writer Alfie Kohn, have lamented the fact that many affluent parents have demanded special programs for their children, sometimes at the expense of both the poverty powerless and other children who do not have the high level of influence enjoyed by their more affluent counterparts.

When the more influential, affluent parents do not have their way, they sometimes leave the public school system in favor of private schools or even home schooling. And the underlying perception around the country is that private schools are "better" which motivates many parents to take their children out of public schools. Unfortunately, many persons define "better" to mean schools which are populated by affluent children, most of whom are European Americans. These children often out-perform their less affluent counterparts in academics. Some parents leave the public schools because of the First Amendment requirement of church and state separation. This amendment has antagonized a large group of American parents from the religious right who argue for certain types of religious instruction, the pseudo-science of "creationism," formal prayer, and other forms of religious activity which are clearly forbidden by the U.S. Constitution.

In order to address these basic issues, interviews were conducted with a cross-section of Americans who responded to questionnaire items. The sampling included both educators and non-educators; persons from a variety of racial/ethnic backgrounds; persons from both affluent and non-affluent backgrounds; people from different geographical locations; persons connected with both public and private schools; and individuals representing different age groups. Responses to the questionnaire items were included in the various chapters.

The term "elitism" was defined as: The practice or belief in control of organizations, society, or any group by persons from the "best," wealthiest, or a "select" group; also membership in organizations which are perceived to be the "best." The term "affluence" refers to an abundance of money or material goods. Translated into dollar amounts, it applies to single people who earn in excess of $80,000 a year or a family of four which earns more than $100,000 a year. At the time of this writing "poverty" was defined by the federal government at about $20,000 or less for a family of four.

Other terms in the book also require specific definitions. We chose not to use the terms "liberal" or "conservative" since they have been cavalierly used in a rather generic sense when referring to persons from the economic, political and religious right and left. In truth, the term "liberal" traditionally has referred to "abundance," "generousness," "open-mindedness," tolerance of a plethora of ideas, and the like. However, many persons from the religious/political/economic right sometimes use the word to characterize people who they feel are nearly sub-human! Thus we have opted for using the terms "right" and "left" when appropriate.

This work is divided into three sections. Section One discusses the pre- and post-Columbian history of the American education system and its goals in a democratic society. Section Two examines the nature of the criticisms and analyzes the motivations of the critics. The final section includes an analysis of the significance of the public education system's possible demise, a suggested plan of action for the improvement of public education, and an epilogue offering some final suggestions for parents wishing to secure the best possible public school education for their children.

Section One: The History of the System.

Chapter One: Discusses the history of American education. The emphasis is on critical multicultural and socioeconomic issues and elitism is a main theme which is carried out in the various episodes and topics under discussion.

Section Two: Who are the critics? What are their complaints? Are they valid? What are the similarities between public and private schools?

Chapter Two: With the issue of elitism as the central concern, this chapter relates to challenges confronting the public education entity from the private sector. What motivated these criticisms?

Chapter Three: A socioeconomic comparison of public vs. private school performance. A major emphasis is on the validity of test-score comparisons and determining whether private schools really out-perform their public counterparts. Reasons for these outcomes are addressed. Educational "equity" is discussed along with the manner in which people decide if a school is "good" or "bad."

Chapter Four: The theme in this chapter is education for "able learners." The question of whether gifted/talented education is elitist is addressed. The work of Alfie Kohn is one of the primary sources of information.

Chapter Five: Multicultural education and its attempt to create equality of equal educational opportunities, a constitutional guarantee.

Chapter Six: Legal issues in connection with the public school criticisms are investigated here. Legal rulings which have antagonized some groups are discussed along with the impact from the establishment clause of the First Amendment.

Section Three: If America's public school system crumbles, so what? A blueprint for action will be included.

Chapter Seven: So what? If our present system of public education falls apart, what difference will it make? If some sort of voucher system becomes legalized, what effect might it have on public education?

Chapter Eight: This chapter will include a blueprint for saving the public schools. It consists of goals for preserving and restructuring the system along with strategies for implementing operational procedures for its improvement.

Chapter Nine: An epilogue consisting of final thoughts.

1

Early Beginnings of American Education

Unlike many other countries, American education is not mentioned in the U.S. Constitution. While there were existing systems of education functioning among the eastern Native American tribes among the Algonquian and Iroquoian language groups when the Europeans arrived, their curriculum was totally different from what had been utilized in Europe. No formal reading instruction occurred in the Americas, which was one difference between education among the North America natives and the European immigrants. The Europeans had the enormous advantage of living closer to Gutenberg, Germany, site of the printing press invention. Consequently, unlike the native residents of North America, many Europeans were becoming literate due to the availability of the printed word and access to alphabets. The first known Native American tribe to become literate was the Cherokee nation. This occurred when they acquired a syllabary through the efforts of Sequoyah, long after the Europeans first arrived.

During the first two and a half centuries after permanent European American settlement, southern colonists were often beleaguered by survival concerns and seldom gave serious thought to the establishment of schools until long after their initial arrival. The colonies have been classified into three distinct groups by historians and the schools which materialized reflected the values and educational needs of the southern, middle, and New England colonies.

SOUTHERN COLONIES

The southern colonies were primarily agrarian and many of the new immigrants from Europe were not prepared for the rigorous life they faced. Jamestown was settled in 1607 and just seven years later, John Rolfe's first shipment of tobacco reached England. The production of tobacco grew rapidly since the product was well received and highly sought after in Europe. The popularity of tobacco in Europe motivated American planters to start up tobacco plantations wherever possible. The success of this crop translated into big profits for southern tobacco growers, but in order to achieve this success and the wealth which followed, a source of cheap labor was necessary. Eventually, this was found in Africa and slavery became an important source of the southern colonies' economy. Consequently, large numbers of Africans, captured by slave traders, were sold to the tobacco farmers in the southern states. A large workforce was necessary to plant, cultivate, and harvest those lucrative crops. West Africa became the primary source of cheap labor for the young colonies as the slave ships sailed to Africa to pick up their human cargoes and sell them to the tobacco growers in the southern colonies. Many came from the present-day countries of Ghana and the Ivory Coast.

Those who survived the terrible ordeals on the slave ships were sold to planters in the southern colonies. However, the quarters on the slave ships were quite cramped and life on these small ships was miserable. Records show that only about half of the captured Africans reached the American shores alive. Many of those who survived the crossing did so because of their physical condition and their luck. Some actually drowned after jumping off the ships, attempting to swim ashore.

The elite aristocracy of the southern colonies consisted of merchant capitalists, who were concerned primarily with making large profits through trade in the markets around the world. Because of their entrepreneurial goals, they were extremely ambitious and driven toward the acquisition of new lands in order to enhance their profits. However, in addition to what seems like self-serving goals, they also believed that they were preordained to serve the state and perform well in their various positions of authority. Many planters served as community leaders.

But while the wealthy planters were in control of the southern political system, not all of them emulated the English gentry. Also, religion in the South did more than provide spiritual outlets. Church going offered a chance to socialize and discuss business issues.

The southern colonies tended to view education as a private matter. Tutors were hired on the plantations in order to provide an education for the offspring of the plantation owners. Little serious thought was given about the need for a common school educational program for all the children. And while the use of tutors was usually reserved for the wealthy classes, there were some charity schools which were religious and philanthropic organizations. In general, there were no educational opportunities available for Native Americans, African American slaves or indentured servants. In general, education was viewed as a commodity which was needed by the sons of the wealthy planters. Their education was often provided by tutors, some of whom had graduated from Yale or Princeton.

The children of the underclass rarely had an extensive formal education. While one reason for this lack of preparation was due to southern attitudes regarding who needed education, another reason was the rural nature of the country which made it difficult to create schools and school districts because of the sparse population.

One of the first strategies for education in the South was the apprentice system which required a young person to work with a master who would teach the child a trade. The problem with this educational ploy was that there was little coordination and planning to ensure that all children mastered basic competencies.

Teaching missionaries also worked with southern children in order to provide them with an education. The Society for the Propagation of the Gospel in Foreign Parts (SPG) contributed more than 300 missionaries to the southern colonies in order to provide an education for low-income European Americans, Native Americans, and African Americans.

The Anglicans viewed education as a responsibility of the parents so much of the instruction was carried out at home. Consequently, education in the southern colonies was primarily a private matter and common schools, funded by the colonies and later the states were slow to materialize. In lieu of a system of common schools, religious organizations founded charity schools, while tutors were often utilized by the wealthy plantation owners.

MIDDLE COLONIES

Historians have sometimes characterized education in the middle colonies as being quite sectarian in nature. There existed a diversity of religious denominations along with a lack of commonality in language and values. Consequently, schools were developed along sectarian lines and little thought was given to the creation of common school systems. During the late 1600s private schools were forming, particularly in the larger cities, such as Philadelphia.

The importance of a practical education was stressed in Philadelphia and William Penn's first and second Frames of Government for the Pennsylvania colony included allowances for public schools which stressed religious instruction and practical skills. However, these schools failed to flourish due to the diverse religious sects. The Quakers and Mennonites provided private religious schools which stressed reading and writing. Reading was taught through the use of the Bible. Other private non-denominational schools commenced to appear during the 18th century, particularly in Pennsylvania.

NEW ENGLAND COLONIES

Since the early Europeans who settled in New England consisted of large numbers of English "Puritans" it was not surprising that they created school models which were employed in the old country. Consequently, three types of schools emerged during the 1630s. **Dame schools** provided instruction for mostly boys and the teachers were usually housewives. Seldom were there any formal "school buildings." Rather, these private enterprises were usually carried on in someone's house.

Other schools were known as **reading and writing schools**. However, more often than not the primary curriculum was reading so that children could learn to read the Bible. Writing was usually not emphasized as much and the schools were established for children from the lower socioeconomic classes. **Latin grammar schools** tended to be of a more scholarly nature and were attended by boys from the higher socioeconomic echelons. The Boston Latin School, purported to be the oldest high school in the United States, was created in 1635 in Boston. Partly supported by public funds, the curriculum was similar to what could be found in the Latin schools of Europe. Classical instruction along with religious studies seemed to be most prevalent. The study of Latin by affluent male students was of paramount importance and many of the graduates of the Latin schools went on to attend Harvard University, the nation's oldest institution of higher education.

Religion dominated the social fabric of other New England schools and their curriculum. The early textbooks such as the "hornbooks" and the *New England Primer* included religious couplets such as "In Adam's fall we sinned all." The Primer also contained prayers and hymns and was the most widely used schoolbook during the 1600s.

One of the early precursors to the development of common schools was the "Old Deluder Satan" Act. Enacted in Massachusetts' General Court, the measure required that schools be established in towns of 50 households or more. Reading and writing instruction was required and instructors' salaries were provided by the inhabitants in general and/or by the parents or masters of the children. Towns with populations of 100 or more households were required to establish a Latin grammar school in order to prepare students for attending Harvard University. The Puritans in the region were interested in perpetuating their religious value systems, and they believed that schools could accomplish that end.

Many of the teachers during the pre-revolutionary era were graduates from Yale University. These young people often attended Yale in order to become missionaries. However, many of them opted for the teaching profession. One example was Nathan Hale. As a young teacher in New England, he taught male students, since women were not allowed to attend some of the early colonial schools. However, he conducted special classes for young ladies on a tutorial basis.

During the Revolution he disguised himself as a schoolmaster in order to spy on the English encampments in New York. He hollowed out part of the sole in his shoe and actually made maps of the British encampments. He was captured just as he was ready to cross the East River back to colonial territory. He was later executed for his spying enterprises.

At this time in American history, the common practice was that any form of organized education was for young European American males. Women, Native Americans, and African American slaves were generally not entitled to participate in organized education programs.

THE AGE OF ENLIGHTENMENT:
EUROPEAN CONTRIBUTIONS

The Age of Enlightenment in the United States covered a period of history from about the early to mid-1700s to the eve of the American Revolution. During this time ideas from Europe were pouring into the young North American colonies. These unique concepts were largely responsible for creating new ways of looking at education. They focused on the nature of humankind, the structure of the universe, and science methodology. This period was also called the Age of Reason.

The Copernican view of a heliocentric universe was a major breakthrough in human understanding of the universe. This corrected the erroneous notion of an earth-centered universe which had prevailed up to that time. Isaac Newton's discovery of gravitation revolutionized the world of physics, and Deism evolved as a new religion which was more in keeping with the many profound scientific discoveries. Moreover, the work of the French mathematician, Descartes, helped lead to new views of learning through use of the scientific method. Also, the Englishman, Francis Bacon, pioneered the notion of inductive logic. Another Englishman, John Locke, argued that at birth, the mind was a "blank slate" which would eventually process information through the life of the learner. In other words, people's ideas were not innate at birth.

In addition to these fresh concepts, Jean Jacques Rousseau championed new ideas about teaching and learning through his classic work, *Emile, ou Traite de l' Education.* His ideas led to the notion that in order to teach children, you must first understand them. Also, infants were born inherently good, not evil. He often gets credit for being the father of "child-centered education" which would influence educators and psychologists such as John Dewey and Carl Rogers much later.

Johann Heinrich Pestalozzi was another key pre-American Revolution Swiss educator who greatly influenced American educational thought. He argued that in teaching young children it was necessary to appeal to them through their senses. He used actual objects, models, and pictures in teaching. Much of his work became embodied in the philosophy of kindergarten instruction.

Isaac Newton's work challenged some of the religious views of the universe when he argued that it could be explained through scientific data. And these secular notions greatly influenced many of the so-called "founding fathers" such as Benjamin Franklin whose ideas became so influential in colonial America. He and others thought that knowledge should be useful as well as meaningful. He went on to propose a liberal view of education which should include instruction in English grammar, composition and literature, classical and modern foreign languages, science, writing and drawing, rhetoric and oratory, geography, history, agriculture and gardening, arithmetic and accounting, and mechanics. In addition, he felt that a sound mind needed a sound body, underlying his belief in the importance of physical activities.

JEFFERSON'S VIEWS ON EDUCATION

Thomas Jefferson also exerted enormous influences on the development of education in the United States. Dominated by the views of John Locke and the writings of French educators, Jefferson was fluent in Latin, Greek, English, and a number of modern languages. When he was just 33 years of age, he wrote the Declaration of Independence and in addition to his two presidential terms, he was a vice-president, minister to France, secretary of state, governor of Virginia, a member of the Virginia legislature, and a delegate to the Continental Congress.

He believed quite strongly that in order for a participatory democracy to "work" it was necessary to provide a vigorous, effective public system of education in order to help citizens make good decisions in the voting booth. He wanted to establish elementary schools which would be supported by taxes. Instruction in reading, writing, and arithmetic would be offered to European-American boys and girls for the first three years. He also advocated twenty other elementary schools for poor European American children who were talented. His high schools would be for European American boys and the curriculum he advocated consisted of English grammar, Greek, Latin, geography, and advanced arithmetic.

As advanced as Jefferson's ideas about education were for those times, it should be noted that girls were not provided the same opportunities as boys; there was no thought given to compulsory attendance; and no provisions were made for the education of African Americans or Native Americans. Moreover, the bills that he proposed in the Virginia legislature were not passed and his pet educational project seemed to be the establishment of the University of Virginia which became his last major contribution to education.

THE FEDERAL ROLE IN EDUCATION

In spite of the urgings of some of the more liberal figures of the time, education was not recognized as a major national concern and no mention of it was made in the new Constitution. Many historians believe that the reason for this was that education was viewed as a function of the church and the parents. Since the Constitution stipulated that powers not held by the federal government were transferred to the states, education commenced to be thought of as a state function. Consequently, until this day, the United States actually has 50 different systems of education.

However, some federal actions have exerted major influences on the educational systems in the states. One of the first such actions was the Land Ordinance of 1785, which mandated a survey of the Northwest Territory. These lands were divided into six square-mile townships which were further subdivided into smaller plots consisting of one square mile in area. The sixteenth plot of each 36-plot township was designated as the plot which supported education through its fundraising endeavors.

OTHER EARLY INFLUENCES

While early education followed a "little red schoolhouse" format, by the early 1800s the ideas of Rousseau and Pestalozzi commenced to take hold in the United States. Instead of the Puritanical notion of the child as a "miniature adult," the work of these two Europeans gradually exerted an influence in the United States. It can also be said that during this period of time, public education in America began to acquire a more secular nature. Teaching materials also reflected this secularized spirit in such books as the *New England Primer* which gradually adapted a softened religious tone. Moreover, the practice of praising England gradually ended and was replaced with references to George Washington and other national heroes.

During this time, the most common type of secondary education was still the Latin grammar school. These schools tended to be primarily college-prep in nature and were usually attended by affluent young European American children. They were mostly private and were not supported by public funds because of a general feeling that tax monies should not be spent on secondary education. Sometimes these secondary schools were referred to as "public" in nature, simply because anyone who could pay the fees could attend them.

After the Revolution, the attitudes regarding secondary education gradually began to change. As academies tended to become larger and more diversified in their offerings, they began to come under the control of state legislatures. For example, in New York, the state legislature had to approve the incorporation of academies. Charters were provided when the requirements were met. This led to a period known as The Common School Movement.

THE COMMON SCHOOL MOVEMENT

After the dawning of the 19th century, the new nation elected a president whose roots originated from poverty. Consequently, much of the pomp which had characterized the previous administrations, suddenly disappeared when Andrew Jackson took the Oath of Office in 1829. In modern terms he could have been known as the "macho" president, given his propensity for wrestling matches and fist fights. During his administration, the movement for common schools slowly began to materialize even though other issues were deemed to be more important. For example, one controversial piece of legislation which occurred during Jackson's presidency was the Removal Act of 1830 which allowed the federal government to re-locate Native Americans to the Oklahoma Territory. This led to the infamous "Trail of Tears," a forced removal of the Cherokees.

About the same time, Harriet Tubman, an African American slave, decided that the search for freedom was of paramount importance. After running away to the North, courtesy of the underground railway, she returned to the plantations in the South, guiding more than 300 African American slaves to their freedom. Some were later forced to flee clear to Canada as a result of the later 1857 *Dred Scott* Decision which ruled that even if African American slaves were able to escape to free territories, they were still the properties of their southern slave owners.

The 19th century saw an increase in poverty as the nation became more industrialized. Its capitalistic economic system required a cheap labor force in order to ensure maximum profits. This situation gradually increased in scope as the demand became greater. While a solid middle class was also emerging, the city slums and the deplorable working conditions for African Americans motivated new demands for public education in the United States.

The fledgling movement for free public schools received much of its impetus from Robert Dale Owens, an early leader in the New York Workingman's party. He advocated an educational system which would eliminate the burgeoning economic stratification in American society. Free public schools became viewed as the ultimate answer for providing a suitable work force for the new nation. The new movement also was motivated by a growing feeling that human beings were capable of reaching their maximum potential if they were properly educated. However, it should be noted that institutional racism also played a role in the evolution of the nation's public school system. Little thought was given to the education of Native Americans and there was a general notion among European Americans that African slaves possessed an inferior level of intelligence and were probably not capable of learning as well as their European American counterparts. Since slavery was the primary source of cheap labor in the South, it was also felt that the children of African American slaves didn't need a great deal of education since they probably would become field hands like their parents. That, coupled with the belief that literacy might cause problems for slave owners, tainted the development of common schools in that part of the country.

Also spurring the development of the common schools was the emerging notion that education was a way to get out of the wilderness. That, combined with a growing humanitarian influence paved the way for the creation of free public schools. Among the prime movers during the common school movement were James G. Carter, Horace Mann, and Henry Barnard.

Carter was a Harvard graduate and legislator who became a teacher and quarreled with much of what he saw in the nation's schools. He ridiculed Massachusetts' first school law as being supportive of lax standards. Finally, as the Massachusetts House chairman on education, he was able to persuade the Massachusetts legislature to create the country's first State Board of Education.

Horace Mann became the first secretary of the Massachusetts Board of Education. He exhibited a humanitarian spirit and became known as an important educational reformer and a prime mover of the common school movement. During his term of office he established the *Common School Journal*, one of the nation's early professional publications for teachers and others who were interested in education. He also set up schools for the preparation of teachers. His annual reports proved to be influential in the other states as well as Massachusetts. In these documents he discussed the need for better school buildings, more knowledgeable school board members, better teachers, and perhaps most importantly, the need for a strong secular system of public schools throughout the land.

Henry Barnard, a member of the Connecticut legislature, exerted his educational leadership in Connecticut and Rhode Island. A Yale graduate, he was interested in many of the reforms of Horace Mann and attempted to carry them out in Connecticut and Rhode Island. Many of his reform ideas came from Pestalozzi, whom he observed in Europe. However, his school reform notions, such as education for women, angered the political right in Connecticut and he was voted out of office in 1842. Moreover, they also abolished the State Board of Education which Barnard created a year after Horace Mann's successful efforts in Massachusetts.

However, he moved to Rhode Island and became that state's first commissioner of education. He also was the nation's first commissioner of education, serving in that capacity from 1867 to 1870. He argued that the wealthy classes should support public education through increased taxes. He believed that such support was in their own best interests. Professionally, he is also known for becoming the editor and publisher of the *American Journal of Education.*

The first half of the 19th century was noted for the creation of tax-supported public schools which were controlled by the state. However, there was vigorous opposition to this concept, particularly in the more rural areas of the United States. One of the key pieces of legislation affecting the concept of tax-supported public education for all was Pennsylvania's Free School Act of 1834 which provided for local taxation and some state aid.

EARLY AMERICAN HIGH SCHOOLS

One of the first public funded high schools in the United States was the English Classical School in Boston. This new high school was actually an academy for boys who were not interested in attending the Boston Latin school which prepared them for enrolling at a university. Soon after, similar public high schools were opened in Portland, Maine, and New York City. These early models were for boys.

However, the most important piece of legislation affecting the development of tax-supported public high schools occurred as a result of the Massachusetts Law of 1827 which required the public support of secondary schools in towns or districts of 500 or more families. In large cities, these schools were required to include Greek and Latin in the curriculum. Soon, the states of Maine, Vermont, and New Hampshire had adopted similar pieces of legislation and by the beginning of the Civil War other urban areas around the nation started their own public high schools.

For obvious reasons, the public school movement plateaued during the Civil War, but the famous Kalamazoo Case, an 1874 U.S. Supreme Court decision, ruled in favor of local school boards taxing citizens for the support of public high schools. This was a landmark decision which provided a constitutional precedent for establishing tax-supported public schools in the existing states and the others which would be admitted to the Union.

POST–CIVIL WAR PROBLEMS FOR SCHOOLS

After the end of the Civil War the South was in ruins. The meager beginnings in the public school movement stood still during the conflict and an impoverished and totally defeated Confederacy was hard-pressed to finance schools since mere survival took first priority. Kept in a state of illiteracy by their owners and southern legislatures, African American slaves, now freed, lacked the educational skills they needed for survival. Moreover, due to the abject poverty with which the southern states were forced to contend, it was totally impossible to fund adequately the two segregated school systems which existed there. And to exacerbate the problem, southern European Americans had generally experienced inferior levels of education compared to their northern counterparts. Many were illiterate and had received inadequate schooling. This further added to the enormous lack of education throughout the South at the end of the Civil War.

One of the bright spots in education during the reconstruction era was the George Peabody Education Fund which was started by George Peabody, a Massachusetts native who had acquired enormous wealth in London. He gained international fame for his philanthropic exploits in the slums of London. One of his main interests was in the area of teacher education. Consequently, he started the George Peabody College for Teachers in Tennessee. At the present time, the teacher education institution is part of the University of Tennessee and has long been considered a pioneer in the preparation of teachers. The school also publishes a journal of education which is one of the finest in the profession.

But, in spite of the attempts to create better education systems in the post–Civil War South, education for freed slaves was meager at best. One of the key figures in the education of freed slaves was Booker T. Washington, a freed slave who became famous for his excellent work, *Up from Slavery*. He was able to persuade backers to finance his school, the Tuskegee Institute, which he started in order to provide an education for African Americans. Opening its doors in 1881, just 16 years after the end of the Civil War, Washington's initial goal was to teach African Americans the vocational skills which would enable them to function in the nation's industrial revolution.

It was a difficult task because of the enormous levels of illiteracy which were foisted on African Americans by Southern legislators and plantation owners. Washington argued that his students would provide northern industrialists with an excellent cheap labor force, a commodity which the entrepreneurs and industrialists simply had to have in order to maximize profits. He also contended that an educated African American population would help the southern economy during reconstruction.

W.E.B. DuBois, the first African American with a doctorate from Harvard, argued that Washington's emphasis on having a vocational school for African Americans helped perpetuate the notion that people with African roots possessed an inferior level of intelligence and could not excel in rigorous academically oriented programs. DuBois also believed that the only way to dispel the myth of African American intellectual inferiority, was to compete on an equal footing with talented European American scholars.

But Washington's counter argument was that his school was located in a hostile, racist environment and that by focusing on a vocational skills curriculum he would not get shut down. He believed in a gradual movement toward the development of a good education for African Americans. Interestingly, he never became a member of the National Association for the Advancement of Colored People (NAACP).

In spite of the efforts of many, education in the South lagged far behind that of the North because of the rampant poverty and racism generated during the Civil War.

SOUTHERN EDUCATION DURING RECONSTRUCTION

Due to the poverty in the South after the Civil War, the development of public education in that region went through continuous difficulties. The problem was particularly difficult for African American students who were forced to attend woefully under-funded schools with ill-prepared teachers. Southern schools were racially segregated as were most other southern institutions and businesses. A key Supreme Court decision in 1896 did not help matters. The *Plessy v. Ferguson* decision centered around the constitutionality of segregated railway cars. An 8-1 ruling determined that racial segregation was constitutional as long as the facilities were equal. So the phrase "separate but equal" again became a prime argument for racial segregation in the South. (It was first introduced as a prime concept in 1850 in *Roberts v. City of Boston*, which legalized racial segregation in Boston schools.) Interestingly, there was one dissenter in the *Plessy* case—Justice John Harlan. In his minority opinion he argued that the U.S. Constitution was "colorblind" and knew no racial distinctions. However, this verdict prevailed for 58 years until the *Brown v. Board of Education* case overturned *Plessy*.

Two years after *Plessy v. Ferguson*, Edward Abbott from Massachusetts led an important Southern educational conference known as the Ogden Movement. The first conference, designed to find ways of improving Southern education, had a strong religious flavor. However the second and third gatherings were more secular and involved a number of important business and civic figures. Receiving support from John D. Rockefeller, Jr., the goal of the 1901 conference was to explore ways which would enable the southern states to move strongly in the direction of free community public schools. The prime mover of the Ogden Movement was Walter Hines Page, an outstanding scholar and dynamic speaker.

One of his key goals was to help the South acquire economic stability through education. He was also a strong believer in the need for better education programs for African American children. He thought that the way to end prejudice against African Americans was through education. At times he even criticized southern people for their right-wing views and their provincialism. Eventually, he was so heavily criticized in the South for his ideas that he moved north. However, his influence caused the South to commence revising their notions about the importance of free public schools for all children.

EARLY PUBLIC SCHOOL CRITICISMS

The inclusion of vocational education programs in the public schools has always sparked controversy. While some right wingers have argued for a curriculum consisting of only the "three r's," others have suggested that a broad-based curriculum including vocational education, history, social and physical sciences, foreign language, physical education, music and art are necessary if U.S. citizens are to assume active roles in the nation's development.

Around the turn of the century the National Association of Manufacturers (NAM) criticized the schools for not exercising the hands as much as the brains. They chastised the schools for failing to include vocational education in the curriculum. NAM lambasted the schools for allowing children to leave school without adequate preparation in the vocations so that they could enter the job market with the necessary skills. These criticisms constituted the beginning of various pressures put on the schools to prepare students for entering the world of work. These pressures would intensify dramatically throughout the remainder of the 20th century.

EDUCATIONAL ISSUES IN THE 20TH CENTURY

Early in the 20th century American cities were growing larger. By 1914 New York City had grown to approximately four million. Less than six decades prior to that time it was under a million! Rapid growth in other cities such as Philadelphia led to new problems. The recent urban residents consisted of European immigrants and rural Americans who left the farms. Since many immigrants were fleeing poverty in their own native countries, many were poor when they arrived in the United States. Consequently, many of them were forced to take up residence in the slum sections of the large urban cities.

This phenomenon often led to strife between different racial and ethnic groups as people at the bottom were often forced to battle one another in order to earn a livelihood. Also, the existing residents sometimes looked down upon the new arrivals with derision. Some immigrants refused to attend English classes, preferring to maintain their native language. Of course, this is still a common criticism and a major problem for schools. While bilingual education programs still exist around the country, some states, such as California, have ended such efforts unless parents demand that their children be involved in them.

Historically, poverty has resulted in lower school performance for children. This correlation is often the result of inferior funding for the schools attended by low-income children, the lack of successful role models for poverty culture students, health and nutrition difficulties, and a host of other socioeconomic factors which all translate into poor school performance.

Often through the nation's history, right-leaning politicians have not been too eager to create federal programs which would meet the needs of American youth from poverty circumstances. However, left-of-center social reformers such as Jane Addams, founder of Chicago's Hull House, established programs which would meet the needs of poor children. She was successful in soliciting the aid of John Dewey and was awarded the Nobel Peace Prize for her efforts.

PHILOSOPHICAL ROOTS OF AMERICAN EDUCATION

The end of America's "Frontier Era" and the urbanization of the nation, had profound effects on the nation's development and the lives of the people. Moreover, the ideas of influential Europeans began to affect the thinking of American educators throughout the land. The country's normal schools prepared teachers for certification and teacher educators became influenced by Johann Heinrich Pestalozzi who helped put Rousseau's child-centered ideas into practice in teacher preparation institutions.

Johann Friedrich Herbart, along with many other educational philosophers such as John Dewey, believed strongly in the importance of motivation in the learning process. He felt that learning became more effective as the students' interest was aroused. This was the first step in his learning model. After the preparation stage (motivation) came the presentation of new material. A third stage, referred to as association, involved relating the new material to older material which had already been discussed with the students. The fourth stage related to generalization or formulating big ideas based on the material presented. The final stage (application) related to applying the big ideas (generalizations) to new situations which the student might encounter in the future.

Another philosopher who turned his back on the traditional notions of a "subject-centered curriculum" was Friedrich Froebel whose work led to the development of early childhood education, particularly kindergarten. He believed that children of kindergarten age and younger should be taught through means of self-development and self-expression. The best way to instruct children was through games, singing, and other creative activities. Another key element of his kindergarten/early childhood philosophy was the structuring of classrooms as micro-societies where children could acquire social cooperation skills.

One of the nation's first kindergartens was established in Wisconsin by Margaretha Schurz, one of Froebel's students. However, it was not until 1873, when William T. Harris, the innovative, dynamic superintendent of schools in St. Louis, established the first district-wide kindergarten program in the United States. This program was based on the philosophical principles of Froebel and became a model for other kindergarten efforts in the United States.

THE TURN OF THE CENTURY AND "HAVES" AND "HAVE NOTS" ISSUES

The beginning of the 20th century also can be viewed as a turning point in American history insofar as the lines between wealth and poverty were concerned. Southerners, in their interest of ensuring that West African freed slaves were kept in positions of subservience, had created schools of a substandard nature. The feeling prevailed that the children of ex-slaves did not need to have access to America's regular schools. About the same time American jazz was born as a poverty music played by poverty people.

A major economic downturn started in 1893. By this time in history, the two-tiered public education system in the United States was becoming clear. School segregation by race and per-capita income levels was clearly in place. And the records have revealed that the amount of money spent on African Americans in their segregated schools was about half of that spent on their more affluent European American counterparts.

But the education of Native Americans and Latinos was not much better since the funds expended on these two minority groups were not much better than the monies which were set aside for African Americans. Thus, it can be seen that by the turn of the century, the two-track system of education for the "haves" and "have nots" was becoming a reality in spite of the "separate but equal" concept which was constitutionally verified in 1896. Thus, it can be said that by the early 1900s the United States generally had subscribed to the notion that a second class education for children of color was morally okay. Moreover, the education of poor European American children did not fare much better, although they were not segregated by race. The constitutional decisions affecting these events will be addressed in greater detail later in the book.

EDUCATIONAL PSYCHOLOGY AND
AMERICAN EDUCATION

Perhaps no other educational issue has provoked more interest than the topic of how human beings think. Prior to the 19th century, much attention was given to the issue of "faculty psychology." Coming out of a Protestant religious tradition, the term related to the notion that the mind consisted of three "faculties": the will, which assists human beings in developing actions of various types; the emotions, affections and passions which exist in all human beings; and the intellect, which allows humans to think and reason.

Europeans, such as Thomas Reid, a Scottish philosopher, believed that the mind was separate from the human body. It was a spiritual entity, and possessed only by human beings. The three faculties of the mind (will, emotions, and intellect) could be trained for use by people as they encountered different issues which needed to be addressed throughout their lives.

During the last half of the 19th century, Charles Darwin's work led to an entirely different notion of the mind. In his view the mind was separate from the body and was affected by evolutionary growth. In order to survive, the mind had to adjust to the changing surroundings.

William James believed that every one of the "faculties" constituted a critical segment of human behavior and human thoughts were more of a total experience which required a unification of all parts of the mind. Thus, in James' view, it was unnecessary to dwell on the notion that that the mind was composed of a number of different elements.

Thorndike, a student of James', agreed with his mentor that the mind was a separate entity. Rather, he viewed it as an organism which responded to the environment. He refuted the notion that the individual was inherently "good" and believed that nature was for people to use for their own benefit in the context of learning. Finally, he believed that education should be used to change human beings for the better and the human mind was the instrument which could help them change their own nature in order to make their own lives and the world better.

Thorndike developed many of his ideas from the study of animals. Through his research utilizing controlled conditions, he concluded that non-human animals learned through the reinforcement of "correct" responses. He refuted the notion of "faculty psychology," arguing that his research concluded that learning occurred through stimulus-response bonds which led to consistent behavior patterns. His work influenced later researchers such as B.F. Skinner who believed that behavior could be modified through the provision of appropriate reinforcements. Skinnerian research in the 20th century revealed that animals could learn to shoot a pingpong ball through a hoop, replicating a successful goal in a basketball game.

The animals received food reinforcements for each successful movement until the behavior was learned. In a similar manner Pavlov, the Russian psychologist, already had taught dogs to drool by ringing a bell when they were hungry and given food. By adequate repetition, the animals learned to drool whenever the bell rang.

As can be expected, Pavlov and Skinner were not without their critics. J.P. Guilford argued that human beings were not pigeons or rats and they should not be taught in the same way. His mid-20th century Structure of the Intellect (SOI) model identified 150 different kinds of human intelligences. Carl Rogers argued that the best way to teach was to help individuals take charge of their own learning and he strongly denounced reinforcement theory as being Machiavellian.

Psychologists interested in child growth and development included Arnold Gesell and Jean Piaget. Gesell spent a good deal of his career observing children in laboratory settings. He helped articulate a clear picture of the role of maturation in child development. He believed that sequential stages of development occurred in children and his ideas gradually became embodied in American educational practices.

Piaget is probably most widely noted for his developmental stages which he embodied in four separate periods: the sensorimotor period (age zero to two); the preoperational period (age two to seven); the concrete operational period (age seven to eleven); and the formal operations period (age eleven or twelve on). His work was instrumental in establishing defendable rationales for curriculum placements throughout the grades.

Alfred Binet and Lewis Terman are often viewed as the "fathers of intelligence testing." Binet was interested in human intelligence in his career as a French physician. Toward the end of the 19th century he had begun his investigations of human intelligence. Early in the 20th century he was asked by the French Minister of Public Instruction to create a suitable instrument which could be used in the identification of students who were lazy or unmotivated and students who were truly deficient mentally. He agreed to create such a test but cautioned that it could not be used as a valid measure of human intelligence.

The American, Lewis M. Terman, learned of the instrument and created his revision of Binet's work in order to measure intelligence. He revised it, had it translated into English, normed it using a population of 1,000 European American, middle-class subjects from Palo Alto, and the intelligence testing movement in the United States was launched.

Critics have argued that this Stanford-Binet scale, and others that followed, contained a strong middle-class/European American bias which created difficulties for students from other racial/ethnic backgrounds, as well as poverty students. That argument still persists.

THE STRUGGLE FOR EQUALITY
IN THE 20TH CENTURY

By the beginning of the 20th century, public education systems in the United States were in place in all 48 states but new concerns were surfacing. The 1896 *Plessy v. Ferguson* case had already allowed for segregated schools. While most of the racially segregated schools were in the South and dealt with the segregation of African American and European American children, segregated schools commenced to appear in the Southwest where Mexican American children were forced to attend schools which were designated as "Mexican schools." Of inferior quality, many of the teachers did not hold regular teaching credentials. Some school districts also segregated Chinese American children.

De Jure school segregation was caused by blatant racism against African Americans, Asian Americans, and Latinos. The substandard schools designated for these minority youth were under-funded and by the first quarter of the 20th century, the two-tiered system of American education was even more firmly entrenched. Ironically, the parents of many of these children helped constitute the cheap labor supply in the agricultural industry. Southwestern states such as California, Arizona, and Texas made full use of their services but the children struggled in school, partly because of the inferior schools they were forced to attend. Hostilities against the minority farm workers surfaced periodically in the form of riots and other acts of aggression. The perception was that these minority farm workers were taking jobs from European Americans. In reality, many European Americans refused to work in the fields, causing farmers to seek out the laboring services of Mexican Americans, Filipino Americans, Chinese Americans, Japanese Americans and others. The ultimate goal for growers was to acquire the cheapest labor possible.

Other examples of the nation's love affair with cheap labor had occurred earlier in the nation's history. Chinese Americans were recruited by Charlie Crocker of Hopkins, Crocker, Huntington, and Stanford, the chief architects of the mid-19th-century Central Pacific Railroad project which created unprecedented growth in the western United States. These laborers also suffered from persecution by some European American groups who were convinced they were taking their jobs. However, they were recruited by Crocker because of their experience as hard-working laborers in China.

By the turn of the century the nation's industrial revolution was in full swing, led by the manufacture of automobiles and other industrial goods. By 1929 there were an estimated twenty million cars on the newly created streets and roads of the United States.

During the first half of the 20th century, American education was heavily influenced by John Dewey who started his famous laboratory school at the University of Chicago in 1896. His work provided a philosophical foundation for the progressive education movement in the United States. Based on Dewey's philosophy, the Progressive Education Association was formed in 1919 to reform public education. Five of its seven principles argued in favor of allowing children the freedom to develop naturally; providing adequate motivation in order to achieve maximum learning; encouraging the teacher to be a director of learning, rather than an information provider; addressing the many factors which affect student learning; and encouraging the school and home to collaborate in order to provide the best education possible. Dewey believed in having students use kinesthetic activities to improve learning and utilize the community in order to maximize teaching efforts.

But Dewey also had his critics. While his ideas were based on sound educational philosophy, some argued that optimum teaching strategies called for more rote learning than Dewey liked. Moreover, some groups did not like the idea that Dewey was interested in individual differences and argued vigorously for a more "demanding" approach based on teacher dominance, rote memorization and the like. Such views were often expressed by right-wing groups such as the John Birch Society, a foe of Dewey's philosophical notions.

RACISM AND SEXISM AFFECT PUBLIC EDUCATION

The development of American jazz can be used to illustrate the rampant racism which existed in the United States during the 20th century. This brand new American art form emanated in the Mississippi delta regions, particularly around New Orleans. Since it was primarily an African American contribution in its early years, jazz was highly segregated racially and considered to be a lower-class art form by many European Americans. Even renown jazz musicians such as Louis Armstrong were not allowed to stay in the hotels where their groups were playing because of the racist attitudes which prevailed at the time. And since African Americans were considered to be second-class citizens, this helped verify the notion that it was also okay for their schools to be both under-funded and of inferior quality.

Another concern during the first part of the 20th century was the education of young women. Historically, there had been a belief that their education was of less importance since they were expected to be mothers and homemakers. Moreover, women were not franchised until the election of Warren G. Harding in 1920. However, the two world wars had helped the public realize the importance of educating young women. And compared to 1900 when only half of the nation's women worked outside of the home, by the end of World War II, one-third of the women over 14 were employed. Moreover, women were becoming a powerful political force, often voting more to the left of center than their husbands.

But no other incident had such a profound effect on American education as the *Brown v. Board of Education* Supreme Court decision in 1954. The ruling of the Warren Court was that schools should become racially desegregated "with all deliberate speed." Both northern and southern schools districts were forced to find ways to carry out the edicts of the U.S. Department of Justice as a result of this landmark decision since racially segregated schools were declared to be "inherently unequal" and consequently unconstitutional, by the U.S. Supreme Court. Moreover, the 9-0 decision helped usher in the nation's "Civil Rights Movement" which had dramatic effects on the nation's schools.

THE INTENSIFICATION OF PUBLIC SCHOOL CRITICISM

During the same period of time, critics of American schools began to surface as a result of the Russians launching of Sputnik during the early stages of the "space age." Books were published with such titles as *Why Johnny Can't Read* by Rudolf Flesch, an Austrian American lawyer and non-educator who nonetheless became a staunch foe of the reading methodology used in American schools. And even military figures such as Admiral Hyman Rickover argued that American schools were inferior to those of the Russians. While most of the critics were attacking public schools, it is important to note that nearly all of the persons responsible for the launching of America's early space efforts were products of the public schools. Nonetheless, this period of time saw some of the first major criticisms of the nation's public school system.

Another vocal critic of American education was Dr. Max Rafferty, a right-leaning superintendent of schools in California who advocated returning to the use of McGuffey's readers in the state's reading programs. Along with Governor Ronald Reagan, the two figures battled with the leaders of the state's k-12 system and California's higher education institutions over educational philosophy and funding issues.

POVERTY: ENORMOUS PROBLEMS FOR PUBLIC SCHOOLS

The inequality of American schools became a political issue during the aftermath of *Brown v. Board of Education*. During the administration of President Lyndon Johnson, a major effort, dubbed The War on Poverty, attempted to provide enabling legislation which was designed to eradicate poverty and assist low-income persons to become upwardly mobile. It was one of the first times in U.S. history that an American president became seriously concerned about the growing poverty and its effects on the nation's schools. The so-called "white-flight" era occurred partly because of the existing racism which motivated many European Americans to flee the public schools and either move to new neighborhoods that were not affected by *Brown v. Board of Education* or move children to private schools which were relatively unaffected by the new desegregation requirements. However, other parents were more concerned about the problems related to poverty, often exhibiting an unwillingness to have their children assigned to schools which were populated with large numbers of low-income students.

During the same period of time the nation also struggled with the problem of providing adequate education programs for Native American children. Historically, the country's paternalistic policies created huge poverty problems for reservation and non-reservation Native Americans.

A partial remedy was attempted as a result of the Indian Education Act (IEA) of 1972. Native American children trailed the nation in school performance. The dropout rate was about twice the national average and the per-capita income level was 75 percent lower than the nation's average. Native Americans had acquired an enormous distrust of the Bureau of Indian Affairs (BIA) by that time.

The IEA attempted to secure more Native American involvement in decision making and required the cooperation of tribes, parents, teachers, and students. The act was amended in 1978 in order to focus on "culturally related academic needs." Tribes were then able to operate their own schools and attain greater control of the IEA-funded programs.

As national criticisms against the public schools intensified, public school educators sought ways to initiate any sort of changes which might produce better learning. Faced with a growing number of low-income students, attempts (sometimes viewed as educational "panaceas") to address these problems were initiated in the schools. Individualized reading, team teaching, "schools without walls," learning centers, and a long list of other ploys were often utilized during the post-Sputnik era. Unfortunately, many of these programs were carried out with no appropriate research efforts which might have verified their effectiveness. Even the popular *Theory into Practice* efforts of Madeline Hunter at UCLA in the late '60s went unresearched for more than two decades when research results finally revealed that her widely utilized teaching/learning model produced no significant differences in student learning compared to other strategies.

THE NATION'S NEW OFFICE OF EDUCATION

During the latter stages of the Carter administration, the democratically controlled U.S. Congress passed legislation which created a new cabinet-level Department of Education. The action had enormous political overtones, motivating President Reagan to argue for its abolishment as part of his presidential platform. Reagan's Secretary of Education Terrell Bell originally thought that this new cabinet-level office of education was not needed and the federal interest in education could best be handled in the original Departments of Health, Education and Welfare. However, after holding that office he saw the importance of having American education under the influence of a cabinet-level body and reversed his earlier stance.

William J. Bennett, a controversial conservative right-wing Republican appointed secretary of education by Reagan, argued for a number of major changes in American education. A staunch foe of bilingual education, a strategy employed to comply with the 1974 *Lau v. Nichols* Supreme Court decision, he argued for the adoption of an "English-only" approach to instruction in the public schools. He opted for a "total immersion" strategy for teaching children whose native language was not English.

Bennett's foes decried his anti-bilingual education stance, arguing that it made no sense to force children who did not understand English to endure instruction in that language. To his critics, such a procedure only meant that children wasted their time in school when they had little notion of what the teacher was saying. Their argument was that the instruction should be in the student's native language when needed. At the same time, the student should be taking English classes, the ultimate goal being to have all students become functionally bilingual.

But to exacerbate the problem, many of the students who were in need of the special bilingual instruction were from developing countries with poorly funded education systems. Many of these children came from low socioeconomic families and had parents who were often not overly literate in their native language. This made it difficult for such persons to provide the kind of instructional assistance their children needed. Many educators argued that this situation made the need for bilingual instruction coupled with English instruction an absolute necessity.

Many of these people were coming to this country to provide cheap labor in order to increase the profits of businesses and corporations. Thus, the public schools, encountering increasing numbers of poor children, commenced experiencing a decline in test scores which angered much of the American public. Of course, the convenient scapegoat was the classroom teacher who was forced to bear the brunt of much unfair criticism.

At the same time, many Americans began to be affected by "downsizing," "restructuring," and "outsourcing," euphemisms for the elimination of many middle-income positions. As this occurred more frequently, the American middle class experienced a decrease in its numbers while CEOs and other upper-echelon, high-income personnel received financial incentives for laying off personnel to increase corporate profits. Obviously, this resulted in decreasing numbers of the American middle class while the percentages of affluent and poor persons escalated. Thus, the socioeconomic structure of the United States commenced resembling a barbell which was thin in the middle and heavily weighted on both ends.

These changes in the American work force were reflected in public school populations. Public schools commenced to experience greater numbers of poverty and dysfunctional students which affected test scores. Since the nation was undergoing an increase in testing, the numbers made it appear that America's teachers were doing an inferior job of teaching because of the declining test scores.

About the same time, the National Committee on Excellence in Education completed a major report on education. Chaired by David Gardner, president of the University of California, the report contained a scathing indictment of American education, referring to a "rising tide of mediocrity," and arguing that major reforms were necessary. The report became heavily politicized with Republicans arguing for voucher systems and less money for public education, while Democrats tended to reject vouchers because they violated the establishment clause of the First Amendment to the U.S. Constitution. Democrats also sought better funding for public schools.

MORE POVERTY PROBLEMS FOR PUBLIC SCHOOLS

The finance issue was well articulated by Jonathan Kozol in his classic work, *Savage Inequalities*. In his book he identifies the problems educators must address because of inadequate funding for schools in low-income neighborhoods. The title of the book suggests that the nation's inattention to the provision of quality public education for poverty children is tantamount to criminal neglect. He cites East Saint Louis as one example of the national poverty problems encountered in public education. Kozol describes problems of under-immunization for young children, sewage backups, school closures due to stopped-up toilets, layoffs of teachers due to a lack of funding, inoperable science labs, broken gymnasium pipes, inadequate computers, and a lack of adequate textbooks.

Sadly, the descriptions of conditions in East Saint Louis are similar to the poverty problems affecting low-income communities throughout the rest of the United States. Deplorable poverty conditions were found by Kozol in Boston, South Chicago, New Jersey, and Washington D.C. Moreover, he found enormous per-pupil funding disparities. For example, New Jersey's average per-pupil expenditures in Camden, were recently $3,538 compared to $7,725 in Princeton!

DO "REFORM" EFFORTS SUCCEED?

Unfortunately, many so-called "reform" efforts are merely cosmetic devices such as more statewide testing, bans on "social promotions," longer school days, and more homework. Early in the year 2000, California's Governor Gray Davis argued in favor of financial rewards for high performing schools. If this plan is carried out, it might mean that high-affluent schools with high test scores become even wealthier!

The growing gap between the "haves" and the "have nots" has led to increasing criticism of the nation's public schools and the problem has become even more politicized in recent years. During the past three decades the nation has become increasingly involved in national and statewide testing programs. This makes it possible to compare the test performance between nations, states, and even from school to school. However, a critical phenomenon that very few politicians and private citizens address is that the preponderance of research studies show that per-capita income correlates positively with test scores. Thus, schools, school districts, and states with small poverty populations continuously score higher than their low-income counterparts. Yet politicians often attempt to "out-reform" each other as they scramble to make political hay out of either high or low test performance. Much more often than not, these reform efforts are based on little or no understanding of sound principles of teaching and learning. And not only do many of the reform attempts not work very well, some of them even get tangled up in legal issues.

For example, private schools have usually been able to recruit outstanding afflu-ent students whose parents can afford the private school tuition. They have also been able to recruit excellent athletes which has sparked much controversy among the public schools. At the time of this writing the Brentwood Academy in Ten-nessee sued the Tennessee Secondary School Athletic Association (TSSAA) as a result of that body's decision to disallow the academy from contacting middle school athletes in an attempt to recruit them to their private high school. The U.S. Supreme Court will rule on the case during the the fall of the year 2000. The acad-emy's attorney fees have topped $1 million since the suit was filed in 1997. The academy filed the suit in response to a fine by the TSAA which accused the acad-emy of making improper contacts with the middle school athletes.

Many young athletes who come from affluent families also have taken to hir-ing personal trainers and athletic coaches in order to make them more marketable for college scholarships and possible professional contracts later. Thus, it can be seen that affluent children have an unequal advantage in athletics as well as in the classroom. Affluence allows parents to choose whether their child attends a public school or a private one. This option is not open to children from low-income families. This means that public schools have no choice but to accept the chil-dren who come through their doors. Private schools can accept or reject poten-tial school candidates. Consequently, public schools are likely to have a great number of students who do not perform well on tests, the primary way of decid-ing which schools are "good" and "bad" in the United States.

Obviously, these factors have led the media, politicians, and the public in gen-eral to believe that public schools are of inferior quality. However, as the research tells us, this supposed inferiority of public schools is little more than poverty affecting school performance in numerous ways. This issue will be addressed in greater detail in later chapters.

At the present time public education is being attacked because of a perceived low level of performance. It is reeling from a "brain drain" of bright, affluent students who have moved their high test scores to private schools of various types. Even so, the public schools still have huge numbers of bright students who score high on test scores. The problem is, their numbers are dwindling and in general the 361 known reform attempts between 1987 and 1997 have done little to convince the public that America's public schools are improving. However, the annual Gallup Polls show that Americans usually award their neighborhood schools with an A or B!

But this suspicion about the quality of public schools has not always existed. Historically, Americans have tended to take pride in the public schools around the country. In the remaining chapters we will further examine the unequal oppor-tunities, discuss the problems of elitism, and offer some suggestions for improv-ing the public schools.

REFERENCES

Alexander, Kern and Alexander, David. 1995. *The law of schools, students, and teachers.* St. Paul: West Publishing Company.

Butts, R. Freeman and Cremin, Lawrence A. 1953. *A history of american culture.* New York: Holt, Rinehart, and Winston.

Chartock, Roselle K. 2000. *Educational foundations: An anthology.* Upper Saddle River, New Jersey: Merrill.

Commager, Henry Steele, ed. 1960. *The era of reform, 1830-1860.* Princeton, New Jersey: Van Nostrand.

Conant, James. 1959. *The American high school today.* New York: McGraw-Hill.

Cubberly, Ellwood P. 1919. *Public education in the United States: Study and interpretation of american history.* Boston: Houghton Mifflin.

Dewey, John. 1916. *Democracy and education.* New York: Macmillan.

Dewey, John. 1899. *The school and society.* Chicago: University of Chicago Press.

Flesch, Rudolf. 1955. *Why Johnny can't read.* New York: Harper and Row.

Fordham, John. 1999. *Jazz.* New York: Barnes and Noble Books.

Furnas, Joseph C., 1598-1914. *The Americans: A social history of the United States.*

Guilford, J.P. 1967. *The nature of human intelligence.* New York: McGraw-Hill.

Gutek, Gerald L. 1986. *Education in the United States: an historical perspective.* Englewood Cliffs, New Jersey: Prentice Hall.

Kozol, Jonathan. 1991. *Savage inequalities.* New York: Crown Publisher, Inc.

Markowitz, Harvey, ed. 1995. *American Indians.* Pasadena, California: Salem Press.

Mitchell, Bruce. 1965. *Nathan Hale: schoolmaster/patriot.* Denver: University of Denver.

McWilliams, Carey. 1939. *Factories in the field.* Boston: Little, Brown and Company.

Randall, William S. 1993. *Thomas Jefferson: A life.* New York: Henry Holt and Company.

Rippa, Alexander S. 1992. *Education in a free society: an American history.* New York: Longman.

Rousseau, Jean Jacques and Foxley, B. trans.1911. *Emile.* New York: Dutton.

Slavin, Robert. 1989. Educational faddism and how to stop it, *Phi Delta Kappan,* June.

Sondheimer, Eric. 2000. To waste court time is supreme stupidity. *Los Angeles Times,* Los Angeles: 5 March.

Washington, Booker T. 1901. *Up from slavery: An autobiography.* Boston: Houghton Mifflin. Reissued Doubleday 1953.

Webb, Dean. L. et al. 2000. *Foundations of American education.* Upper Saddle River, New Jersey: Merrill.

2

Who are the Critics and Why?

Throughout history, European Americans have always been critical of governmental institutions. Indeed, one of the motivating factors for Europeans making the dangerous earlier trips to the "New World" stemmed from the many irritations people had with the crown heads of Europe. Indeed, chastizing the government has become a great American way of life. For example, Woodrow Wilson was criticized for being too cerebral; Franklin Roosevelt was accused of being too far to the left; Ronald Reagan was vilified for being too far right and Bill Clinton was excoriated for being a womanizer. And the nation's public schools have also attracted more than their fair share of criticism. Seemingly, criticism has become an American way of life!

THE EARLY CRITICS OF PUBLIC SCHOOL EDUCATION
IN AMERICA

Even such well-respected early school reformers such as Horace Mann (discussed in chapter one) did not escape criticism. Often referred to as the "Father of American Education," Mann became a spokesman for the nation's Common School Movement. Elected to the Massachusetts legislature in 1827, he was instrumental in the creation of Massachusetts' system of education. He also established one of the nation's first state boards of education in 1837. At that time he gave up his legislative position and became involved in public education on a full-time basis.

He used his position of secretary of the Massachusetts State Board of Education to further his commitment to the cause of common school education. A prolific writer, Mann created a number of reports to the Massachusetts legislature

which outlined his ideas of good educational practices and sound teaching principles. The reports also included a number of recommendations for improvement.
They were made available to other states and early in the nation's public education system, Massachusetts became known as a leader. The reports became influential in developing guidelines for creating good common school systems in
other states as well as Massachusetts.

Mann fought vigorously for the support of the public school movement in
Massachusetts. He derided the antiquated, often unsanitary school facilities and
fought for the inclusion of modern school equipment. In addition to his interest
in improving common schools and educational practices, he also argued for better teacher education and battled for improving the status of the teaching profession. Because of his efforts he was successful in persuading the Massachusetts
legislature to make substantial improvements in the financial support of the
Massachusetts common schools. He was also able to create three teacher preparation institutions (then known as Normal Schools) in the state of Massachusetts.

However, Michael B. Katz questioned Mann's motivation and actually provided a slightly different interpretation of Mann's notion of the "Common School
Movement." Katz believed that all Mann wanted was to develop a working class
of United States citizens who would become young workers for the country's
fledgling factories. Katz argued that what the nation was trying to do in its education programs was to train and recruit young labor-market candidates to adapt
to the country's need for trained citizens to become available for factory positions. These jobs did not require a high level of sophistication but literacy and
a minimal level of mathematical prowess were necessary. Thus, Katz accused
Mann of wishing to establish a common school program to serve these purposes.
These criticisms centered around the presupposition that the business interests
influenced the early common school movement for self-perpetuating reasons.
Thus, the perception of some early common school movement critics was that
they wished to foist education on a relatively "uninterested in education" working
class of people.

As described briefly in chapter one, James Carter was another educational
reformer and one of the early common school reformers. Paving the way for
Horace Mann, he wrote a number of newspaper articles which argued in favor
of a common school effort which would rely on the use of public tax funds. He
railed against the public apathy which mitigated against a strong system of public school support and he lamented the gradual decline of the struggling common school philosophy in the United States. He warned that unless new
legislative actions occurred, the common schools might totally disappear by the
middle of the 19th century.

Carter actually paved the way for the work of Horace Mann through his
efforts in the Massachusetts legislature. His ideas on educational reform were
finally successful in persuading the Massachusetts legislature to create the first
bona fide State Board of Education. Such boards exist in nearly all states at the
present time.

HORACE MANN'S REFORM EFFORTS CRITICIZED

But other critics of the new reform efforts soon surfaced. Mann was accused by religious leaders such as Frederick A. Packard, secretary of Philadelphia's American Sunday School Union, of being an atheist. And Mann's admonishments in favor of religious freedom were lambasted by some right-leaning ministers in the colonies. In fact, since Mann was viewed as being "nonsectarian" he also was viewed as godless by such critics.

Another interesting educational controversy during the first half of the 19th century centered around comments made in Mann's legislative report of 1843 praising the Pestalozzian philosophy which was prevalent in Prussian schools. Mann described his impression of the classroom rapport and mutual respect which existed between teachers and students. He reported that he heard no teacher ridiculing, scolding or verbalizing negativism toward the students. However, a group of Boston principals issued a rejoinder to his observations and reiterated their beliefs in corporal punishment and "strict" discipline.

In addition, Mann was attacked by religious leaders for his defense of religious freedom. Ironically, Mann was a deeply religious man himself, even though he believed that religious indoctrination had no place in the schools. However, he argued that the Scriptures could play an important role through the reading of the Bible without comment in the schools. For displaying this attitude, Mann was attacked as being "godless." He was unmercifully attacked by pseudo-religious politicians and religious leaders.

These incidents serve to illustrate the early beginnings of the continuous attack on the common schools by various religious factions. One of the problems stems from the fact that one of the reasons for the early European migrations to the "New World" was to escape the religious oppression which had existed in Europe. However, it is interesting to note that many of the persons who had escaped this "old world religious oppression" seemed to be intent on imposing their own religious dogmas on their new environment! Of course, this would lead to interesting new problems in the United States since the nation's constitution strictly prohibited a state religion as a result of the First Amendment's establishment clause which was enacted in 1791.

NATIONAL EXPANSION IN THE MID-1800s

Between 1830 and 1860 better than one million acres of land became part of the United States. As the westward expansion began, the perception that common schools were necessary became intensified. The California gold rush resulted in a new interest in moving west. The California region had not been explored by Europeans until then because of the failure of Juan Cabrillo and other European explorers to locate any gold or spices in that portion of the Americas. However, in 1842, gold was first discovered in California by Francisco Lopez near the present-day city of Santa Clarita and the major discovery occurred in 1848 in Sacramento. These findings caused a flood of adventurers to travel to the Pacific regions to seek their fortunes.

CRITICS OF TAX-SUPPORTED PUBLIC SCHOOLS

But other criticisms of the Common School Movement soon surfaced. Some people argued that the wealthy should not be required to pay for the schooling of others. After all, the argument went, we made our money and can afford to pay for our own children. So, why shouldn't others do the same? During much of the first half of the 19th century, many persons, particularly in the South, believed that education was still a family matter and families should "take care of their own." This philosophy was most pronounced in the southern and midwestern regions of the new nation.

In fact, it was the gold discovery of 1848 that would change California forever. John Marshall has been credited with the gold discovery in 1848. It was the year of the Treaty of Guadalupe Hidalgo in which California became part of the United States following the end of the Mexican War. Up until that time, the state had been part of Mexico and Spain who took the land away from the original Native American inhabitants. Of course, with these changes and the huge influx of settlers racing to the gold fields, came the need for schools.

One of the early figures who pioneered the development of that state's school system was John Swett who was instrumental in securing passage of some of California's early school laws. Other influential figures elsewhere in the United States were Caleb Mills in Indiana and Calvin H. Wiley in North Carolina. Mills wrote articles promoting the notion of public-funded school systems in Indiana while Wiley's influence in North Carolina helped change the attitudes of southerners who historically had resisted the notion of tax-supported public schools.

Resistance to the notion of tax supported free public schools was also strong during the early portions of the 19th century. As this westward expansion of Europeans commenced, the need for education followed and the argument for tax-supported public schools prevailed. Some of the resistance came from German Americans who migrated from a nation where public schools had often been "pauper" schools for poor children. Thus, the notion of public tax-supported public schools which were open to all was foreign to them.

Working-class people often viewed the public schools as an instrument which could be used to protect them from the tyranny of the elite. They were perceived to provide a mechanism where the children of the working class could acquire an education and become upwardly mobile. Consequently, persons from this socioeconomic group were usually in favor of developing free public schools which were financed from tax dollars.

On the other hand, some groups of affluent Protestants viewed public schools as instruments of social control through which the dominant English-speaking Americans could exert control over the lower socioeconomic classes. Moreover, public schools could be a valuable instrument for forcing all Americans to use English and establish a curriculum which espoused a philosophy of Protestant Christianity.

THE CIVIL WAR AND AFTER—
NEW SCHOOLING DEVELOPMENTS

By the middle of the 19th century more than half of the nation's children were enrolled in public schools, particularly in the western, northern, and midwestern states. However, as stated in chapter one, the southern states lagged in the development of public education systems at the outset of the Civil War. Following its completion, they were hard-pressed to establish such systems due to the terrible devastation suffered by the Confederate states.

America's Industrial Revolution created an intensified demand for a system of public education. The enormous industrial growth following the Civil War exacerbated the demand for skilled workers and business and industry increasingly looked for the American education system to help out. Gradually, the notion of free, tax-supported public schools gained stronger support and toward the end of the 19th century, more than twice as many students attended public high schools as the private academies which had been so popular up to that time.

The public high school had became even more solidly entrenched as a result of the famous Kalamazoo case of 1874. This ruling meant that local school districts could levy taxes for the support of both elementary and secondary schools. The landmark decision also squelched the old argument that public funds could not be used for secondary education. The ruling paved the way for the spate of compulsory attendance laws which followed. By 1910 all the states had established compulsory attendance requirements even though the public school criticisms still persisted.

At the end of the Civil War, the illiteracy rate in the nation was surprisingly high. African Americans were generally denied the opportunity to become literate and southern European Americans also had a high level of illiteracy due to the slow development of public schools below the Mason-Dixon line. Schools were racially segregated, particularly in the South, because of legal mandates. But segregated schools also existed in some northern regions due to *de facto* living patterns. Also, segregation in the South affected virtually all human institutions such as transportation systems and hotels, and even drinking fountains and rest rooms. The constitutionality of these practices was finally tested in the landmark *Plessy v. Ferguson* case of 1896 (briefly mentioned in the last chapter).

PLESSY V. FERGUSON AND RACIAL SEGREGATION

Homer Plessy was 1/8 African American and 7/8 European American. He was able to "pass" (for "white") and so he would ride the "whites only" railroad car since it had superior facilities to the cars for "coloreds." A passenger recognized Plessy and reported him to the conductor for being on the wrong car. The conductor had Plessy arrested when he refused to leave the car arguing that he was mostly "white." The case reached the U.S. Supreme Court which upheld the Louisiana segregation law, arguing that it was "separate but equal." Not only did the decision uphold segregation (as long as it was "equal") but it also established that a person who had 1/8 "Negro" blood was a "Negro."

However the case had another spin to it. John Harlan, the lone dissenter and author of the minority opinion, argued that segregated facilities led to the development of a racial caste system excluding African Americans from associating with European Americans. Because European Americans held the power and wealth in the United States, the doctrine of "separate but equal" relegated African Americans to an inferior position.

Nonetheless, the nation finally had a constitutionally verified rationale for creating racially segregated facilities throughout the country. It was clearly one of the United States' most blatantly racist acts and it served to drive a further wedge between the "haves" and the "have nots." It also signaled other American institutions, such as the schools, that racially segregated schools were declared to be within the guidelines of the U.S. Constitution, and therefore legal. It also caused some to believe that acts of racism were constitutionally acceptable.

Moreover, it had the effect of paving the way for other kinds of segregation in the schools. For example, the San Francisco schools decided to establish racially segregated schools for Chinese American students and "Mexican schools" were created for Latino students. These segregated facilities for non-European American students were of inferior quality and helped widen the gap between low-income citizens and their more affluent European American counterparts. However, it is important to remember that great numbers of European Americans have found themselves in poverty as well.

But Harlan's dissenting opinion stirred the passions of many social critics who were interested in addressing the meaning of the Fourteenth Amendment to the U.S. Constitution. The 8-1 opinion related to school segregation during the waning days of the 19th century. And while Harlan was merely one voice in the wilderness, his dissenting opinion sparked much debate among Americans. The Plessy trial forced many people to ponder the morality of such practices when the topic had been relatively ignored since the early days of segregation. The issue was debated with increasing passion throughout the 20th century. Many foes of integration were delighted with the opinion. But the true significance of the decision would not hit until halfway through the century. However, some stalwart segregationists vowed that they would remove their children from the public schools if they were ever to become integrated. Thus, the Plessy decision helped pave the way for a large group of public school critics who would under no circumstances allow their children to attend racially integrated public schools. This attitude became one of the key motivational factors for the anti-public school attitudes which became so prevalent during the last half of the 20th century.

Much of the evolving segregation following *Plessy*, was *de facto*, meaning that people chose where they wanted to live. So, as people selected their residence areas, many of their choices had something to do with economic factors. People with common income levels tended to congregate in certain neighborhoods. Racial factors also entered into human decisions regarding various life pursuits and the attending salaries that people could enjoy in the neighborhoods of a given community. Such living arrangements also have been designated *de facto*, since in some parts of the country there were no legal mandates which forced people from different ethnic/racial groups to live in certain locales.

In the South, most of the school segregation was of the *de jure* variety. The term comes from the Latin and relates to racial segregation that is required by law. The fact that schools for African American students in the South were woefully under-funded led to the legalization of unequal educational opportunities based on race. The fact that such schools were of very poor quality because of their under-funding motivated some Americans to become critical of segregated public schools for African Americans in the South. However, the concept of "guilt by association" gradually led some Americans to view all public schools in the same light. Thus, the ranks of the public school critics began to grow in numbers.

THE "MONKEY" TRIAL AND MORE RELIGIOUS CRITICS

Few trials in American history aroused the passions of the American people as the famous "Monkey" trial pertaining to the role of evolution in the nation's public schools. It all started with the publication of Charles Darwin's *Origin of the Species* in 1859. Darwin's notions of evolutionary growth conflicted with the traditional Calvinistic ideas about "original sin." Darwinian theory tended to emphasize individual differences in humans while encouraging the concepts of child development which portrayed young children in a different light. Previously, Calvinistic dogma had focused on the notion of original sin, thus placing the new Darwinian theory into conflict with the traditional right of center religious philosophy. Moreover, the new Darwinian ideas of evolution centered around the belief that it was necessary to structure classroom activities in a context investigating problems in a rapidly changing world. This infuriated traditional Christians who had adapted a more rigid approach to teaching and learning, emphasizing rigid discipline and an unchanging environment.

The controversy led to the famous Scopes trial of 1925, which took place in Dayton, Tennessee. It related to the First Amendment of the U.S. Constitution which centered around the separation of church and state. John Scopes, a Tennessee biology teacher, taught the theory of evolution to his students in violation of a Tennessee law which prohibited this practice.

The contentious issue pertaining to Darwin's theory of evolution pertained to human beings and simians having common ancestors who were involved in an evolutionary process in the creation of human beings. This idea infuriated the religious right, since Scopes insisted on including evolutionary theory in his biology course. The case was argued by William Jennings Bryant and Clarence Darrow, an equally eloquent lawyer, who defended Scopes.

The essence of the trial was the articulation of two distinct points of view. Darrow argued for Scopes, claiming that he merely utilized scientific, humanistic biological theories of evolution. On the other hand, Bryant claimed that the schools should adhere to the Judeo-Christian biblical interpretations of creation. While Scopes "lost" the trial, he was only fined $100.

The significance of the trial is that anti-public school sentiment was rekindled because of the religious issues. The fact that the religious right had subscribed to the William Jennings Bryant position exacerbated the argument between the scientific community and right-leaning religious figures who rejected the position of Charles Darwin. The argument persists to this day.

Of further interest is that the trial occurred shortly after the end of World War I. In that conflict the scientific prowess of the United States had a great deal to do with the outcome. The fact that Bryant felt science must be stopped, was counter to the opinions of the persons most closely connected with that conflict. The people believed in science and didn't want it squelched or even altered a great deal. As a result of the trial the religious right became more vocal in their complaints about schools.

PRE–WORLD WAR II EDUCATION CRITICS

Other critics of American education were about to surface as a result of John Dewey's influence. While many of the criticisms described thus far have come from the "religious right," Dewey's critics came from more secular backgrounds. One of his most famous books, *The School and Society*, was based on three lectures that he delivered at the University of Chicago Laboratory School. He elaborated on his ideas of the emerging new roles in education. He argued that public schools must take on many of the educational tasks which once occurred in the home. In his other lectures he went on to criticize the traditional schoolroom because of its uniform curriculum and its resistance to insisting that curriculum and instruction be based on a "child-centered approach."

He argued that schools must cease operating like factories and a closer connection should exist between the experiences of children and the more structured content of the various disciplines. He railed against a rigid curriculum which failed to take into account the rich and highly individualized experiences of children. He championed the ideas of individualized instruction and argued that it made little sense to have all children working on the same thing at the same time.

So, for Dewey, problem solving was the key element in the thinking and learning procedures for young children. Moreover, Dewey referred to education as a "process" rather than a "product." Instead of education being a "preparation for life" it was life itself. Interestingly, he was one of the few educators who had the luxury of seeing his ideas become part of the general public education philosophy during his lifetime.

CRITICS OF JOHN DEWEY

However, the critics soon attacked many of his educational ideas. Perhaps the key element of his educational philosophy was that the goal of a good education system was to prepare children to become fully functioning humans in a democratic society. While this sounds like a noble objective with no negative aspects, some critics believed that his philosophy was too left leaning since the primary focus in teaching and learning centered around the individual student as a potential participant in a democratic society. Not only did his notions antagonize some of the more right-leaning political elements, even members of the education profession objected to his argument that students required highly individualized instructional approaches in order to meet the needs of individual students most effectively.

Moreover, some critics argued that his philosophy was responsible for a "spoon-fed" approach to teaching and learning which taught children that they didn't need to conform to rigid standards of schooling since the ultimate goal was to meet the needs of individuals. Such critics were fearful that this approach could cause school children to become lazy in their learning habits.

Along with his colleagues, such as Ella Flagg Young, a professor of pedagogy at the University of Chicago, his work led to the formation of the Progressive Education Association (PEA). Formed in 1919, the PEA was created around seven primary beliefs about education:

1. The child should be given the freedom to develop naturally;
2. Interest provides the motivation for all work;
3. The teacher should be a guide in the learning process, not the task master;
4. The scientific study of pupil development should be promoted by the refocusing of information to be included on school records;
5. Greater attention should be given to everything that affects the child's physical development;
6. The school and home should cooperate to meet the natural interests and activities of the child; and
7. The Progressive School should be a leader in educational movements.

The famous *Eight Year Study* conducted by the Progressive Education Association concluded that students who attended progressive education schools achieved at a higher level and were better adjusted socially than their non-progressive education counterparts. But the criticisms persisted and the anti-Dewey faction which wished to maintain the old "factory system" approach to teaching and learning mistook many of Dewey's progressive ideas and wanted to return to the old days of rote memorization, recitation, endless drills, and rigid classroom structure.

But in spite of these critics, the public schools still tended to be viewed in a positive fashion. The country's military forces which prevailed during World War I, the pre–World War II recovery from the Great Depression, and the country's success during World War II had all helped to perpetuate the relatively positive image of the nation's public schools. However, the second half of the 20th century would be quite different.

20TH-CENTURY CRITICISM GROWS

A number of critical events which occurred during the second half of the 20th century did not bode well for public education in America. Two non-winnable wars, the American Civil Rights Movement, the War on Poverty, increasing criticisms of public education from the Republican Party, and the growing power of the religious right, all caused difficulties for public education.

One of the country's greatest technological successes helped to achieve victory during World War II. Indeed, the creation and use of two atomic bombs signaled that the United States was the world leader in harnessing nuclear energy. However, the Union of Soviet Socialist Republics (USSR) quickly emerged as a formidable challenge to the technological leadership of the United States. When the Russians successfully launched their Sputnik in 1957, criticisms of the nation's public schools intensified.

Admiral Hyman Rickover chastised the public schools for not teaching math and science effectively. Rudolph Flesch thought that the public schools were not teaching reading properly. Maxwell Rafferty, a right-leaning California superintendent of public instruction also railed against what he perceived to be a lack of phonics instruction in the public schools and argued for the return to McGuffey's Readers. These were some of the more well-known critics of the schools and their criticisms tended to be of a secular nature.

Unlike the aforementioned critics, James B. Conant, in his famous 1959 Conant Report, argued in favor of the large public high school and pleaded for the consolidation of small high schools and school districts into larger units. However, in this report, he also argued that the first duty of parents was to support their public schools and to insist that boards of education set policies and leave professional educators alone so they could get the job done properly.

Answering the critics of public education were reformers such as Jerome Bruner (mentioned in the last chapter) who argued that any subject could be taught in some intellectually honest form to any child at any stage of development. He also believed in the importance of going beyond factual information in the instruction of young children so that they could learn how to grasp concepts and principles.

Interestingly, the work of Maria Montessori, an Italian physician and educator, figured into the public school criticism equation. As the nation moved into the second half of the 20th century, parents who were interested in what they perceived to be a more rigorous type of schooling for their children during their "preschool" years sometimes opted for "Montessori schools." While Montessori differed with Froebel in numerous ways, the two both subscribed to the notion that children possessed an inner force which stimulated their behavior. Ironically, Montessori's early efforts were focused on a poverty section of Rome in which she established a school for preschool children from the culture of poverty. Little did she know that she would attract a large following of parents from the more affluent sectors of the United States.

The strong points of her approach included a strong emphasis on allowing children to progress at their own individual rates, her use of educational games which were designed to teach learning concepts, and her emphasis on sensory education as an important learning device for young children. Moreover, she was one of the first educators who took seriously the importance of providing strong educational programs for young children from low-income circumstances.

But while her interest in individualized education is certainly applaudable, she was accused by some for not paying more attention for the need of young children to acquire social interaction skills which can only be developed through various kinds of group activities. Nonetheless, her private schools became quite fashionable alternatives to public schools in the United States.

BACKLASH FROM *BROWN V. BOARD OF EDUCATION*

One of history's greatest problems for public schools occurred because of the landmark *Brown v. Board of Education* case in 1954. This 9-0 Supreme Court decision had the effect of overturning the 1896 *Plessy v. Ferguson* decision which verified the legality of "separate but equal" schools. With this decision the courts ordered the integration of American schools "with all deliberate speed." Segregated educational facilities were declared to be "inherently unequal" by the U.S. Supreme Court.

One of the first major tests of forced integration occurred at Central High School in Little Rock, Arkansas over the protestations of Orville Faubus, Arkansas governor. President Dwight D. Eisenhower was forced to send in federal troops to integrate the school. Sadly, this episode was only the first in a large number of similar incidents. However, the encounter sent a clear message to the American people. Racially segregated schools were inherently unequal and therefore unconstitutional. They simply had to become racially integrated.

Unfortunately, a number of schemes were initiated in order to circumvent the forced integration edict. Most of them were found to be unconstitutional, including a scheme to fund private schools at taxpayer expense. Many southern parents commenced sending their children to private schools in order to maintain their impassioned beliefs of racial segregation. However, these persons tended to be more affluent then their public school counterparts. This is one of the chief factors which led to a decline in public school test scores. As the more affluent children opted for private schools, the per-capita income levels of public education students dropped.

As this occurred, President Lyndon Johnson initiated his famous War on Poverty. Unfortunately for about 25 percent of the nation's population, the post–World War II prosperity had passed them by, resulting in low-income poverty circumstances for many American children. To compound the problem, many of these children were from non-European American backgrounds. And while education was perceived as a device for leading people out of poverty, many European American parents recoiled at the idea of having their children attend school with poor children who were not "white." Eventually, this led to more public school criticism and an increasing number of parents who commenced opting for private schools.

During the Nixon administration (1969-1974), many solid education programs were either terminated or cut back severely. This right-leaning administration reduced or ended the funding for many of the educational efforts which appeared during the Kennedy and Johnson administrations. Consequently, many of the educational endeavors to address the needs of low-income students suffered severe cutbacks. Moreover, the Office of Civil Rights budget was slashed and Nixon's right-leaning Justice Department did not aggressively enforce civil rights plans. Also, this administration retreated substantially from the "war on poverty" initiated during the Johnson administration, and the enforcement of the 1954 *Brown v. Board of Education* non-segregation Supreme Court decision was also less aggressive.

Under the Carter administration (1977-1981) the education expenditures improved and the Department of Education became a cabinet position. However, a decline in Scholastic Aptitude Test (SAT) scores continued as an increasing number of poverty students were included in the testing pool. Many parents of low-income students were looking for the courts to deal with the problem. This phenomenon helped motivate a "back to basics" movement which erroneously assumed that the schools had stopped teaching the "basics."

THE 1980s: INCREASED ATTACKS ON PUBLIC EDUCATION

The election of Ronald Reagan marked the beginning of a difficult decade for public education in America. Campaigning on a right-wing platform, the Reagan years ushered in a return to politics which had not been seen for many decades. Reagan fought for a decrease in federal expenditures for public education, and he blamed much of the social unrest of the '60s and early '70s on the nation's public schools. His right-leaning National Commission on Excellence in Education referred to a "rising tide of mediocrity" in the public schools and argued that if an unfriendly nation had inflicted such a faulty system of public education on the United States it would have been viewed as an act of war! Needless to say, this rekindled the public's concerns about the effectiveness of public education and helped to generate a renewed exodus from public to private schools.

During the Reagan years the Republican Party moved farther to the right as Republicans aggressively courted the "religious right" which they needed in order to win elections. Consequently, the anti-public school sentiment which was generated during this period of time intensified the interest of right-leaning parents to leave the public schools in order to have their children attend private schools which were perceived as being superior to their public-school counterparts.

Another phenomenon of the '80s and '90s related to the burgeoning new interest in private religious schools. The Reagan disaffection with the American public schools helped motivated many parents to reconsider the possibility of placing their children in private religious schools. While many people did so because of religious reasons, others made the change because "good schools" became equated with school which had very few children of color or low-income students. Unfortunately, few people understood what the research revealed over and over: a high level of correlation exists between the per-capita-income level of students and their test scores. Simply put, high socioeconomic populations get high test scores.

But another problem emerged during the Reagan administration. One of his goals for the year 2000 was to have drug-free schools and to have all American adults become literate. Unfortunately for the nation's public schools, more citizens were convinced of the supposed inferiority of the public schools which led to the development of more private schools, particularly with a religious right philosophy.

The Republican Party's strong position of support for private schools led to an interest in so-called "voucher systems" which would provide parents with financial assistance for placing their children in private schools. This practice historically had been viewed as unconstitutional, a clear violation of the establishment clause of the First Amendment to the U.S. Constitution. This amendment, established in 1791, declared that: "Congress shall make no law respecting an establishment of religion, or prohibiting the free exercise thereof; or abridging the freedom of speech, or of the press; or the right of the people to assemble, and to petition the Government for a redress of grievances."

HOME SCHOOLING ISSUES

In addition to the pressure for public funding of private schools, public schools were forced to deal with a number of issues pertaining to the growing interest in "home schooling." This practice had become more popular with parents who for variousreasons had become dissatisfied with the public schools. In theory, parents would become surrogate "teachers" and create schools within their homes.

Home schooling is another form of private education and offers another alternative to public school participation. By 1998 more than one million American children were being home schooled. Obviously, some of these efforts have been quite successful, while others were miserable failures. All 50 states allow home schooling in different forms. However, the extent of quality control ranges from Montana, which merely requires parents to evaluate the quality of their own home instruction to North Dakota which requires that home-schooling parents possess a teaching certificate and Arkansas which requires home-schooling parents to have a college degree. The requirements of North Dakota and Arkansas have withstood court challenges at the time of this writing.

ARE VOUCHER PROGRAMS CONSTITUTIONAL?

The constitutionality of voucher programs is questionable at this time. In March 2000, Florida's statewide voucher program was declared to be unconstitutional by a Florida circuit court judge. Republican Governor Jeb Bush has promised an appeal and if that fails, he will attempt to secure private funding for the state's voucher program. Before prevailing in Wisconsin's Supreme Court, Milwaukee's voucher program lost two challenges and the U.S. Supreme Court refused to hear the case, letting the program stand intact. But given the right-leaning tilt of the nation's highest court, it is conceivable that it might rule in favor of voucher programs by a 5-4 decision. However, that remains to be seen. But, as things now stand, voucher programs which allow attendance in private schools certainly constitute an imminent threat to the nation's public schools.

OTHER ISSUES FOR PUBLIC EDUCATION

Another battle being fought at the present time relates to curriculum topics and areas of philosophical emphasis. The multicultural education efforts, started after the end of the American Civil Rights Movement, posited that since America is a pluralistic society and becoming more so, it is necessary to create new teaching strategies which are more effective for children from non-European American backgrounds.

Moreover, classroom teaching enterprises should help students acquire a more tolerant view toward the nation's diverse populations. Obviously, part of such an effort requires a more thorough job of helping ALL students become more familiar with and learn to appreciate the various American microcultures.

Unfortunately, many right-wing religious/political organizations have fought this practice. Instead of addressing the issue of cultural pluralism and how it should be dealt with in the classroom, some right-leaning groups have argued for a more "Eurocentric" approach to teaching and learners. Prominent right-leaning figures such as William Bennett, Diane Ravitch, Arthur Schlesinger Jr., and E.D. Hirsch have maintained that instead of utilizing multicultural education approaches we should focus on more Eurocentric positions in teaching and learning. And the debate rages.

CRITICISMS FROM ELITIST FACTIONS

Finally, elitist attitudes in general have constituted a major form of criticism against the American public school. Since elitism is a characteristic generally associated with affluent persons, and since involvement in business pursuits is one of the best ways to acquire wealth, it stands to reason that the American business community seems to be one of the primary sources of influence among the affluent critics. In fact, Lee Iacocca, in a 1991 address to the Association for Supervision and Curriculum Development (ASCD) told the visiting educators that . . . "your product needs a lot of work, and in the end it's your job." He went on to talk about the growing number of poverty students in the United States, creating an interesting metaphor which argued that . . . "your customers don't want to hear about your raw materials problems, they care about results."

However, Iacocca failed to address the obvious point. His company can monitor its "raw materials" and reject materials of poor quality. Public schools can't do that, nor should they. However, this mentality serves to illustrate one of the inherent dangers in allowing big business to influence public education too much. American business has a point of view which may not understand the different kinds of problems which educators must address compared to American business. Iacocca's metaphor proves it.

Educators have dealt with critics before. They will in the future. However, never before have the critics been so wealthy and powerful. And never before have the critics come from such diversified sources. And never before have the public schools been so vulnerable. And as the bright and talented children of wealthy and powerful parents continue to opt for private schools, the problems for public school educators continue to intensify.

REFERENCES

Bell, Terrel, H. 1992. Reflections one decade after a nation at risk. *Phi Delta Kappan*, 74: 592-597.
Binder, Frederick M. 1974. *The age of the common school*. New York: John Wiley & Sons.

Brown v. Board of Education, 347 U.S.483 (1954).

Cubberly, Elwood P. 1948. *The history of education.* Cambridge, Massachusetts: Riverside Press.

Chartock, Roselle K. 2000. *Educational foundations: An anthology.* Upper Saddle River, New Jersey: Merrill

Conant, James B. 1959. *The American high school today.* New York: McGraw-Hill.

Cremin, Lawrence A. 1982. *American education: The national experience.* New York: Harper and Row.

Dewey, John. 1899. *The school and society.* Chicago: University of Chicago Press.

Edwards v. Aguillard, 482 U. S. 578, 107 S. Ct. 2573, 96 L. Ed. 2d 510 (1987) 44.

Gutek, George L. 1997. *Historical and philosophical foundations of education.* Columbus: Merrill.

Katz, Michael B. 1968. *The irony of early school reform: educational innovations in mid-nineteenth century massachusetts.* Cambridge: Harvard University Press.

Moffett, James. 1994. On to the past: Wrong-headed school reform. *Phi Delta Kappan,* 75-8: 584-590.

Plessy v. Ferguson, 163 U. S. 537, 16 S.Ct. 1138, 41 L. Ed. 256 (1896).

Rippa, Alexander S. 1988. *Education in a free society.* New York: Longman.

Webb, Dean L., et al. 2000. *Foundations of American education.* Upper Saddle River, New Jersey: Merrill.

Wildavsky, Ben. 2000. Vouchers lose in school. *U.S. News & World Reports,* 27 March.

3

Are Private Schools Really Better?

As previously stated, the nation has seen a gradual movement from public school participation to enrollment in a number of different types of private schools. In addition to this movement away from public school enrollment, many parents have opted to home school their children. While much of this has to do with dissatisfaction with the legal issues which determine many public school policies and procedures, there is also a perception that public schools simply aren't as "good" as their private counterparts.

FIRST AMENDMENT ISSUES

Much of the dissatisfaction has to do with the First Amendment guarantees of church and state separation. Probably no single issue has troubled parents who profess to adhere to fundamentalist religious principles any more than the prayer in school issue. Obviously, children are free to pray by themselves whenever they see fit. However, the establishment clause of the U.S. Constitution clearly prohibits teachers, school personnel, or others from leading students in prayer. This was clearly articulated in the landmark case of *Engel v. Vitale*, 370 U.S. 421 (1962).

In this case, a board of education ordered a non-denominational prayer to be said aloud each day in the presence of a teacher. The prayer was composed by the New York State Board of Regents which was attempting to comply with a state law enacted by the New York legislature. Children who did not wish to participate in the prayer activities were excused.

Parents challenged the constitutionality of the state law and and the action of the school district which ordered the recitation of this prayer. Even though participation was voluntary, the U.S. Supreme Court ruled that not only organized prayer but also Bible reading were both unconstitutional and, therefore, clearly illegal. In short, the state must remain neutral about religion and refrain from promoting any form of its many doctrines. But while that sounds final, some states such as Alabama have persisted in attempting to skirt the so-called establishment clause of the First Amendment. But, the findings of the *Engel v. Vitale* case were verified in *Abington School District v. Schempp* and *Murray v. Curlett*, 374 U.S. 203 (1963). States, schools, and teachers may not hold religious services in the public schools.

These Supreme Court decisions have clearly upset many parents who are Christian fundamentalists. And since the public schools legally are unable to initiate Bible reading, prayer, and other activities in their schools, many parents who disagree with the constitutional guarantee of church and state separation have taken their children out of the public schools and enrolled them into the various private schools which represent their religious right beliefs.

Not surprisingly, parents who can afford to pay the private school tuition usually come from relatively affluent families. Granted, not all students who attend private religious schools come from wealthy families, but a skewed proportion do. Also, parents who have opted for this alternative to public school involvement often have been forced to transport their children to their new private religious schools since bus services are not always available. Often this has meant that the parents have been able to afford this kind of private transportation.

Moreover, parents who feel strongly about their children receiving education with a strong fundamentalist philosophy are determined to see that their children receive what they perceive to be the best education possible. This usually translates into strong school performance by the children because success expectations tend to be high.

The movement away from the public schools has also become politicized. When Ronald Reagan was elected president, the Republican Party courted the religious right with great vigor. As a result, this group also became an important cog in the election of Reagan and George Bush. As a result of their involvement, the Republican Party moved even more to the right as the GOP openly courted their involvement and made platform concessions in order to keep them in their party. For example, the Republican Party has vigorously fought for voucher programs which would use federal funds to reimburse parents for their children's tuitional tuitional expenses for attending private religious schools.

DISSATISFACTION WITH THE "LOCK-STEP" APPROACH OF THE PUBLIC SCHOOLS

However, parents also commenced taking their children out of public schools in favor of private school placement for other reasons. Some complained that the public schools reflected the old "factory model" with rigid grade-placement systems based solely on age. Other concerns centered around the use of letter grades which were based solely on performance comparisons with other students. Some felt that the public schools had strayed too far from teaching children how to think creatively and to focus more heavily on the acquisition of higher-level thinking skills. Many of these people also opted for private schools, although in much smaller numbers. This particular movement reached its peak in the '60s and early '70s.

At that time, such schools rejected many of the traditional organizational schemes in favor of individual progress plans which were pioneered at the UCLA Laboratory School under the leadership of John Goodlad. This strategy allowed students to progress at their own rate. The curriculum was highly individualized and many of these progressive schools reflected the philosophy of John Dewey, Carl Rogers, John Holt, and others. Some school districts, such as the Goleta Union School District in Goleta, California, had district-wide in-service training programs in creative thinking development. Experimental research studies revealed that such efforts produced significant changes in creative thinking development. However, most efforts of a similar nature were found in private schools at that time.

Other popular private school options were the Montessori schools, patterned after the work of Dr. Maria Montessori in Rome. Her schools were originally established for the purpose of providing education for poor children between the ages of three and six. They came to her Children's House which was actually a school within her own home. Montessori's program stressed sensory training through the manipulation of three-dimensional objects and letters of the Italian alphabet. She believed that this strategy would lead the children to self discovery and eventually a love of learning. She subscribed to the same learning philosophy of Carl Rogers, that is that nobody can teach anybody anything. Rather, learners must learn by themselves. Therefore, she saw teachers as motivators rather than persons who were in charge of "teaching" people things.

Montessori's approach was especially designed for young children because she believed so strongly in the importance of having them acquire a love of learning and a thirst for knowledge at a very early age. Little did she know that her teaching philosophy would become so popular in the United States.

ELITIST REASONS FOR LEAVING THE PUBLIC SCHOOLS

While the exodus from public schools commenced fairly early after the termination of World War II, it finally peaked in intensity during the Reagan/Bush administration and afterwards. Much of the public school criticism was motivated by Secretary of Education William Bennett, who was appointed to his post by President Ronald Reagan. As the second secretary of education, he used his post to denounce the nation's public education system as a failed enterprise.

Due to the enormous popularity of Reagan, many people in the country believed his rhetoric. But Bennett, a trustee of the American Legislative Exchange Council (ALEC), actually paid the bills in order to get a report by this organization to the media. The report, titled *The Report Card on American Education 1993*, claimed that the states with the highest student achievement "tend" to be states that don't spend much money on public education. The report contained no scholarly research data but, nonetheless, Bennett claimed that there was no correlation between the amount of money spent on public education and actual school performance. Opponents of Bennett's claim argued that his views were based on his political opinions rather than research evidence.

But partially due to the great popularity of Reagan and Bennett, this and other anti-public school pronouncements which Bennett articulated had a dramatic negative effect on young Americans with school-age children. Since many of these more affluent young people with school-age children were becoming right-leaning Republicans, they believed the inferiority rhetoric and commenced taking their children out of public school in favor of private school placement.

These actions, coupled with the increasing concern about public school safety, morality, and religious issues, contributed to an era in which more and more affluent parents commenced removing their children from public schools. Indeed, the perception became so acute that some parents who were products of the public schools themselves, placed their children in private evangelical schools which adhered to philosophical positions with which the parents didn't even agree. For example, many of the religious right schools taught creationism in their "science" classes, even though creationism is not based on scientific data but religious beliefs.

While the private Catholic parochial schools were fairly reasonably priced after World War II, some of the fundamentalist Protestant schools charged steep tuitions, putting them out of reach for some middle-income clients. However, given the robust economy in the '90s, affluent persons were willing to spend the money to have their children attend private schools. Also, some Catholic schools started lowering their class sizes which sometimes were as much as high as 60 per teacher after World War II. This class-size reduction resulted in much higher tuition costs which meant that only relatively affluent families could send their children to such schools.

EFFECTS OF *BROWN V. BOARD OF EDUCATION*

But another reason for movement from public to private schools occurred after the 1954 *Brown v. Board of Education* Supreme Court ruling. Since segregated schools were unconstitutional, school districts commenced integrating their facilities in a variety of different ways. This caused many European-American parents to send their children to segregated private schools for European-American children because of their unwillingness to have their children attend schools with children of color. Many of these parents were reasonably affluent.

Thus, the trend for affluent parents to send their children increased dramatically during the last quarter of the 20th century. This perpetuated the argument that private schools in the United States were becoming increasingly elitist in nature since they attracted children from high-income families who typically outperform their low-income counterparts academically. The high test scores from these affluent private school students caused many parents to assume that this phenomenon occurred because of the "superiority" of private schools when the real reason was affluence.

It has been posited by many educators that the reason for the decline in public school test scores has been partly due to a "brain drain" which has seen large numbers of affluent high-scoring children moving from public to private schools. And the correlation between per-capita income and test scores has been strong. For example, when the state of Washington began their statewide testing program in the '70s, they conducted scholarly studies to determine the correlations between variables such as per-capita-income/test scores, class size/test scores and the like. Interestingly, the only two variables which correlated significantly were per-capita income and test scores. In short, schools and school districts with high levels of affluence out performed their low per-capita income counterparts. While this certainly is not news to anyone, it is important to understand the reasons for such occurrences.

WHY DO AFFLUENT STUDENTS PERFORM BETTER IN SCHOOL?

In order to address this issue, it is probably best to examine the obstacles experienced by low-income children. These problems frequently mitigate against good school performance. These difficulties generally result from the effects of attempting to survive on extremely limited incomes. Not enough money simply means that many poverty families are unable to provide the same level of food, clothing, shelter, and health care that is usually enjoyed by affluent Americans. Perhaps the greatest damage of all comes from inadequate diet and health care.

Often, pregnant low-income mothers simply don't have the money to provide adequate prenatal diets for their children. If the problem is too severe it could mean that infants are born with brain cell damage which could well be irreversible. Of course, such a condition translates into poor school performance. Inadequate health care for the mother obviously can cause problems for the fetus. Consequently, when the children are of school age, they may already be experiencing an obstacle which might be too difficult to overcome.

While inadequate diet and poor health care are often overtly recognizable, other factors may be more subtle. For example, children from poverty circumstances typically live in crowded conditions which might have a negative effect on completing school assignments and the like. Often there is no adequate place to study and complete school work. Overcrowdedness also tends to mean more noise which has a further negative effect on home study. Consequently, children from low-income families sometimes are unable to successfully complete assignments on time. But in addition to that problem, the parents are likely to have been products of poor educational experiences themselves. Thus, they may not view the schools as something that will benefit their children greatly. Also, there's a strong likelihood of ego weakness, which is sometimes passed on to the children.

Poverty homes are also lacking in adequate role models. A greater probability of poor school performance exists for children interacting with adult figures who have been ineffective themselves. These adult figures are sometimes unemployed or in careers which are low paying, requiring only meager levels of training and/or experience. Thus, some children may acquire the idea that occupations which require high levels of education may be unattainable for them.

Another factor relates to simple geography. As discussed earlier, some anthropologists believe that there's a relationship between the distance people's ancestors lived from Gutenberg, Germany (where the printing press was invented) and the time in history when they began to read. Obviously, any activity such as reading does not become highly valued overnight. It usually requires several generations for a new behavior to appear in a given culture and then become an integral part of the value system. Thus, not until literate Europeans came did Native Americans commence to read. Obviously, when they were originally subjected to the curriculum of the European American–dominated schools they were at an enormous disadvantage because reading behavior was not yet an integral part of their culture. The abject poverty to which they were subjected after the arrival of the Europeans created a double jeopardy for them.

African Americans suffered in a similar manner. Captured in western Africa, African Americans arrived in this country to find themselves in a position of subservience. West Africa was also a long way from Europe and reading had not yet caught on in that part of the world when all this was happening. So the concept of translating symbols into sound and meaning was a new idea for them as well. To exacerbate the problem for African Americans, they, too, lived in abject poverty as slaves and were forbidden to learn how to read by law or because of plantation edicts. Consequently, at the end of slavery, most were illiterate. No reading role models existed to any degree. (Interestingly, a large number of European American southerners were also illiterate at this time.)

The plight of Latinos was also similar. Mexican Americans provided the United States with its most important source of cheap labor during the 20th century. Moving north from Mexico, they brought their language and their poverty with them in hopes of improving their lives economically. Mexico has been forced to contend with a system of education which is similar to that found in the other developing nations around the world. In short, that has meant students could expect a 6th-grade education, but very few Mexican pupils were able to acquire much education past that point. Moreover, like the African Americans and other non-European American school children their 81 schools were dramatically under-funded and ill-equipped financially to provide students with the quality educational programming found in schools with large numbers of more affluent European American children. Thus, due to the poverty of the people and the language issues, Latino school children were forced to contend with the same kinds of educational shortcomings as African Americans, Native Americans, and other microcultures which did not have access to the advantages enjoyed by the more affluent European American students.

For all poverty groups, the lack of objects in the home can sometimes retard language development. There may not be as much parental guidance in vocabulary and concept development. Because poverty parents work hard and may have less time and stamina after long work days, there could be a greater reluctance on the part of parents to read to their young children and help them acquire concepts of color, shape, size, space, directionality, positionality, and the like.

But in addition to the issues of poverty, language, and health, other socio-psychological reasons also account for the discrepancies in school performance between the "haves" and the "have nots" in the United States. Sociologists often refer to the concept of "instant gratification" which relates to the practice of rewarding yourself whenever something good happens and takes your mind off your troubles. This practice has often led to unwanted pregnancies, drug abuse, and alcoholism, all examples of "instant gratification." It also has to do with the tendency for low-income people to live in the present tense. Many people don't want to dwell on the past because the memories are too painful. Moreover, the future will probably bring more of the same misery, so let's try and not think about it either. What does that leave? The present.

Finally, the economic hardships lead to children having fewer life experiences. If you're financially challenged, you don't plan trips to Disneyland or the beach, let alone Europe. Thus, school-age children from the culture of poverty simply have not enjoyed the breadth of life experiences as their affluent friends from wealthy American neighborhoods. Consequently, they have a much smaller "world view" than their more affluent counterparts. For example, when one of the authors went to the Los Angeles Harbor to board a whale-watching/harbor excursion boat a few years ago, he discovered that only 25 percent of his students in a low-income Los Angeles Unified School District school about one mile from the water had ever been there before!

On the other hand, the same author knows of two primary-school age middle-class boys who have traveled 1,500 miles to go fishing in a pristine glacial lake, two other elementary-age children who have had lessons in a combined total of 10 music and recreation areas, and a high school senior who has already been to most of the United States, Europe and New Zealand, and is an accomplished musician with a scholarship to college because her parents could afford to pay for her music lessons for more than 10 years.

As a general rule children like these are much more likely to have enjoyed excellent health care and interacted with more positive role models compared to their less affluent schoolmates; have been taught how to plan for the future by their parents; have been to museums, libraries, beaches, mountains, other, states, and foreign countries as well; have received multiple lessons in skiing, golf, tennis, foreign language, music, etc., and have experienced more of the world than their poverty-powerless classmates.

So, by the time these two groups of pupils reach the schools, students from affluent backgrounds have acquired an enormous advantage in learning experiences which translates into school success, high test scores, scholarships to prestigious colleges, and all the rest. Considered in this light, it is really quite amazing that low-income students perform as well as they do in school. But, sadly, most Americans don't understand the learning nuances of the affluent and the low-income students. Since it's more likely that the low-income group will be enrolled in public schools, the American public unwittingly makes the erroneous assumption that some students don't do well because they're in public schools and public schools aren't as good as their private rivals. One of the Native American responders to the authors' survey summed it up well when he said that . . . "I believe that public schools are doing the best job of educating everyone who attends school. There is no quality control on the raw material the teachers have to work with. Public schools take everyone."

On the other hand, consider the enormous advantages which the nation's more affluent children enjoy. Having access to the best health care to be found anywhere in the world, they are less likely to enter school with physical problems. The majority have had the extra advantage of attending upscale pre-school programs and have received positive modeling from their parents. These parents have usually been willing to spend great amounts of time reading to their young children who have also seen their parents reading. Consequently, reading becomes a natural activity for them.

In addition to the advantages of early literacy, affluent children have received the powerful message about the importance of becoming well educated. After all, becoming well educated is more likely to help young people gain access to the "American dream." Often parents have commenced planning for their children's college education before they are even born! Moreover, the parents are often not willing to settle for college degrees in a state university or mediocre private college, but have in mind prestigious schools such as Stanford, Massachusetts Institute of Technology, Johns Hopkins, Princeton, Yale, Harvard, CalTech, and a host of other high scholarship institutions.

Consequently, the enormous advantages of children from affluent families seem quite apparent. That some children from low-income circumstances are able to excel and acquire good educations is most remarkable in light of the conditions just described. Moreover, sociological studies are revealing that unfortunately, the gap between affluence and poverty continues to grow.

SCHOOL PERFORMANCE BETWEEN
THE "HAVES" AND "HAVE NOTS"

In light of the sociological/physchological/physiological comparisons between affluent and low-income students just described, it is not surprising that in general, affluent students out-perform their low-income counterparts as revealed on test scores and the other educational assessments used by educators. As previously stated, these differences surface in comparisons of communities, school districts, and even states. In short, the per-capita income level seems to dictate probable school performance. Since affluent parents can afford private school tuitions, it is not at all surprising that private school students tend to out-perform students from public schools. However, as can be expected, there are many exceptions, some of which will be described later.

When comparing the differences between states, it can be seen that a high correlation between the wealth of the state and the test scores of students becomes apparent. The states of Mississippi, Louisiana, New Mexico, West Virginia, Arkansas, Texas, and Kentucky have the greatest percentages of children between the ages of 5 and 17 who live in poverty circumstances (Mississippi being the highest). On the other hand, the states with the smallest percentages of persons between 5 and 17 who live in poverty are New Hampshire, Connecticut, Alaska, Maryland, New Jersey, and Hawaii (New Hampshire has the lowest percentage).

In examining the results of mathematics test scores for 4th- and 8th-grade students, Mississippi, Louisiana, Alabama, California, South Carolina, and North Carolina had the lowest scores (Mississippi being the lowest). States with the highest 4th- and 8th-grade math scores were New Hampshire, Iowa, North Dakota, Wisconsin, and Minnesota (New Hampshire was the highest). Thus, the close correlation between poverty and test score performance can be seen. Mississippi and Louisiana have the greatest poverty problems and the lowest test scores. New Hampshire had the smallest poverty rates and the highest test scores. (Results are based on the reports from the U.S. Department of Education.)

However, statistics can be deceiving and other factors besides per-capita incomes enter into high and low test scores. Some people are in temporary poverty as opposed to being mired down in the culture of poverty for several generations. Just because someone has a financial setback and is classified as being in poverty for one year does not mean that the children automatically commence performing far below the norm.

And the reverse is also true. Children from hard-core poverty families in which parents win the lottery and acquire instant wealth do not automatically start scoring in the top ten percent range on all their tests. But general trends persistently reveal this correlation between per-capita income level and test score results, the public school's most common measure of school performance.

Still, another variable affecting test scores relates to language factors. Throughout history, human beings have felt strongly about the language they speak because language is one of the factors which defines people's ethnicity. Therefore, many people have been reluctant to change their language. Historical exploitation in North America and Africa has resulted in permanent language changes for many.

For example, in the United States, hundreds of Native American languages existed before the arrival of the English speaking Europeans. Because the English eventually dominated militarily, English became the nation's primary language. In a similar manner, Spanish became the language of Mexico and most South American countries.

However, economic issues have complicated the language factor even further. Historically, the United States has relied on cheap labor sources to maximize profits throughout the nation's capitalistic history. In addition to African slaves, Mexicans and other immigrants have also become major sources of cheap labor. In spite of various legal rulings which have attempted to equate the opportunities of all Americans, these groups have consistently lagged behind the European Americans educationally and economically.

And while the end of slavery revealed that most African Americans had become English speakers, many Mexican Americans were not. Since Mexico has continuously struggled economically, the public schools in that country have been woefully under-funded, placing severe limitations on the education available to the nation's children. For some Mexican American school children, the situation creates a double jeopardy since a skewed percentage are below the poverty line, and English is a second language which often causes educational problems. In short, the combination of poverty and language limitations is often a powerful deterrent to effective learning.

Obviously, children from such circumstances rarely are able to attend private schools due to severe financial limitations. And while some private schools provide limited scholarships for low-income children, others do not. Consequently, this means that private schools have a greater number of affluent students who tend to receive high grades and score high on achievement measures. Thus, the probability that private schools seem to be academically superior is high. However, it must also be remembered that when analyzing groups of school children from the same microcultural backgrounds as far as socioeconomic factors are concerned, there are few differences in performance between private and public schools.

For example, in the state of Washington, the Mercer Island School District historically has had both the highest per-capita income level and test scores that equal or surpass the most elite private schools in the state. On the other hand, one of the poorest per-capita income school districts is Toppenish which has large percentages of low-income Native American and Latino students. Their test scores are among the lowest in the entire state.

However, it should also be pointed out that other factors are also instrumental in the private versus public school controversy. Advocates of voucher programs have consistently argued that competition between private and public schools is healthy. However, it should be emphasized that many private school advocates consistently vote against the funding for public schools since private school supporters are usually forced to pay for their private school tuition. Whenever these anti-public school factions acquire sufficient numbers, it becomes very difficult to fund public schools at the local level. Consequently, if the state provides insufficient funding at the state level the public schools suffer.

In the Los Angeles Unified School District, some high schools compete in the Academic Decathlon, a competition in which students must master 10 disciplines at a college level. In a given year, students might be expected to compete in topics such as fundamentals of art, art history (including such topics as Baroque art, Cubism, and Romanticism), music fundamentals, 20th-century musical composition (with 18 specific composers, their styles and genres), the novel *Jane Eyre*,

various works , mathematics
(algebra throug ics of moving
bodies; the pol essay writing;
impromptu pu FTA, multina-
tional corpora rade, and other
relevant issue hout the nation
compete annu chool, a public
high school i El Camino High
School is loc eld High School
and Belmont ly. Both of these
schools are l e school district.

While the m to "go against
the grain," t t scores occurred
in a South C nown as The Ten
Schools Pr the basis of low
CTBS test

Third-gr 15th percentile in
reading an cent of the project
participant ere Latinos. Virtually all the

The go h percentile or better in five ded school year, the
use of gra for "high-risk" students, spe tors, parent involvement and al programs, booster
clubs and sisted of IBM's Writing to Re ies, Saturday enrichment cli in English activities
(PEP), s

Unfo chool which did raise
its score chool performance are
importa eady become familiar
with th haracterized by abject
poverty ate role models, over-
crowded homes, prostitution, alco...........,   Grief management was
necessary in order to meet the counseling needs of children who had seen so much
violence due to drive-by shootings and other acts of violence.

Sadly, many Americans merely find out whether a school is "public" or "private" in determining whether it is "good" or "bad." A great deal of stereotyping goes on. Events such as the school shootings in Colorado and Oregon feed the stereotype of public school violence which is harbored by so many Americans. These actions, coupled with the difference in test scores also have caused many parents to opt for sending their children to private schools, assuming that the education is "better" there. But is it really?

#1   05-11-2005 3:04PM
Item(s) checked out to WESTGERDES, VALER
TITLE: Unequal opportunity : a crisis in
BARCODE: 0140606043507
DUE DATE: 06-08-05

TITLE: Remaking America's three school s
BARCODE: 0140605632391
DUE DATE: 06-08-05

In the authors' survey one respondent, a retired chemistry teacher, noted that "Private schools have the luxury of excluding children who don't fit in. Public schools don't. Private schools have children from affluent families who have often had the luxury of acquiring essential pre-learning experiences which are usually not available to children from poverty backgrounds." Private schools are also more apt to have children from European American families and such persons control the wealth and power in the United States. (In this regard, we should remember that all of our presidents and vice presidents, with the exception of Vice President Curtis who was part Cherokee, have been European American males along with an enormous preponderance of corporate CEOs.)

But while private schools may be safer and have a higher proportion of children from affluent families, it must be remembered that with very few exceptions, private schools do not have the resources to accommodate special needs children who may be hard of hearing, partially sighted, physically disabled, retarded, etc. Nor do they typically have nursing and other health care facilities. A retired Latino school administrator pointed this out in the authors' survey.

Unfortunately, the fact that a skewed proportion of children in high poverty schools around the nation have been and still are children of color, has piqued the latent racist proclivities of many European American parents which sometimes motivates them to seek out private schools which are more likely to be racially segregated. And while racial segregation is an issue which has plagued public schools since the 1954 *Brown v. Board of Education* Supreme Court decision, private schools in general have not worried too much about school integration.

GLARING INEQUALITIES

Obviously, all of the issues addressed in this chapter relate to the central theme of this book which is whether unequal educational opportunities in America are leading up to a national crisis. A recent report by the Applied Research Center in Oakland, California disclosed "glaring inequalities" in the nation's public schools. Native Americans, Latinos, and African Americans are tragically under-represented in college and university programs as well as school programs for the gifted and talented.

The under-representation of these groups in higher education may be partially due to the ravages of poverty which affect such persons disproportionately, and partly due to the demise of affirmative action programs throughout the country. Also, there seems to be a resurgence in white racism (as seen in the termination of affirmative action efforts). White racism seemed to surface when European American Atlanta Braves pitcher, John Rocker, was introduced in Atlanta following his suspension for making remarks about people who were different from him. When he took the mound he was given a resounding standing ovation. This demonstration of support by a mostly European American baseball audience would seem to endorse his unfortunate remarks. Consequently, this display could easily be interpreted to mean that many European American people still harbor racist attitudes which are just below the surface.

It might be correct to assume that many Americans do not really care about the "glaring inequalities" reported by the Applied Research Center's report discussed earlier. Or it might be that many Americans don't seem to care about that issue as long as it doesn't affect them. But the content of the report has to concern Americans who are interested in upholding constitutional guarantees of equitable treatment. While officials from the U.S. Department of Education did not comment on the report, they have acknowledged that a wide gap in achievement existed between European Americans and Asians compared to African Americans, Native Americans, and Latinos.

The 12 school districts used in the studies were large, urban and suburban areas which were racially diverse. Among the school districts studied were Los Angeles and San Francisco Unified districts, and school districts from Denver, Boston, Chicago, Columbia, South Carolina, and Providence, Rhode Island. Among the most alarming findings were the data from the San Francisco Unified School District which revealed that while African Americans comprised 18 percent of the student population, they accounted for 56 percent of the suspensions and expulsions. Disparities between socioeconomic groups in the area of advanced placement and gifted/talented programs will be discussed in a later chapter.

THE GROWING GAP BETWEEN RICH AND POOR

As everyone knows, the United States is the richest nation in the world. With the recent breakup of the Soviet Union, it is also the most powerful. Yet, enormous disparities in wealth also exist. For example, Bill Gates, the world's richest man, is said to have more money then several dozen of the world's poorest nations. But abject poverty exists among African Americans in rural Alabama and Mississippi (as well as the large inner cities), European Americans in rural and urban America, Native Americans on reservations and urban areas, and Latinos in the barrios of San Antonio and other southwestern cities. Sadly, these are only samples of the embarassing poverty conditions which afflict many regions of the world's richest nation.

But how did it get that way and how does it affect children in school, particularly in terms of public-private school comparisons? During the Reagan-Bush years, the decade of the '80s, the number of poverty children in the United States increased by two million. Numerous sociological reports reveal the continuing growth in the numbers of wealthy and poverty people along with a diminishing middle class. Among the reasons brought forth for this problem have been the decreasing influence of unions which offered financial protection for many Americans, and changes in the tax codes which favored the wealthy.

These growing inequities have created enormous problems for low-income Americans in the areas of health care, housing, and the like. The United States still is the only western nation without a national health care program. While countries such as Canada, Norway, and Sweden offer excellent health care for all, the United States does not. Politically, health maintenance organizations (HMOs) have poured tens of millions of dollars into advertising campaigns in order to ensure that national health care programs do not surface. The escalating costs of prescription drugs has motivated some people to go to Canada or Mexico where such items are more affordable. Persons without the means to reach these two countries often have been forced to go without their medication.

The red-hot economy and the robust stock market during the '90s has also contributed to the growing gap. Educated persons with access to the Internet have often become affluent day traders. But not everyone is in a position to become engaged in this and other new occupational areas which produce unheard of affluence. Many persons who have recently acquired wealth have commenced sending their children to private schools, convinced that they are "better." This has resulted in affluent people taking less interest in the nation's public schools with diminished levels of support. If the trend continues, could the nation's public school system become a pauper system?

But the question of whether private or public schools are really "better" has created complicated questions. Unfortunately, "best" in America often relates to who's the richest. As discussed earlier, private school students, in general, come from wealthier families. Public school students do not (of course with numerous exceptions). Some people define "best" as relating to safety. Private schools are usually located in "safe" neighborhoods. The Ten Schools Project schools, just described, do not. National polls continuously reveal that American people like their neighborhood schools but they are highly suspicious about how "good" the others are. However, there is a prevailing notion among most Americans that private schools are safer and "better."

The issue of educational equity seems to be far more important than arguing whether private or public schools are "best." The U.S. Constitution requires that children have access to "equal educational opportunities." This was one of the central themes in the 1974 *Lau v. Nichols* Supreme Court decision which related to equal educational opportunities. The Supreme Court ruled that indeed Lau did not have access to the constitutionally guaranteed equal educational opportunity because his language was not the language used in the schools. In terms of dollars spent per student, Jonathan Kozol, in his 1991 book *Savage Inequalities*, reported a per pupil range of $2,000 to $20,000! And even though equal educational opportunities are "guaranteed" by the Constitution, it seems quite clear that this simply is not happening in America's public schools.

REFERENCES

Alexander, Kern and Alexander, David. 1995. *The law of schools, students, and teachers.* St. Paul: West Publishing Company.

Alexander, Kern and Alexander, David. 1998. *American public school law.* Belmont, California: Wadsworth.

Berliner, David C. and Biddle, Bruce J. 1995. *The manufactured crisis: Myths, fraud, and the attack on America's public schools.* Reading, Massachusetts: Addison-Wesley.

Chartok, Roselle K. 2000. *Educational foundations: An anthology.* Upper Saddle River, New Jersey: Merrill.

Chase, Phil. 1998. Academics: Public schools beat private. *Los Angeles Times*, 21 March.

Coleman, James S. 1990. *Equality in education.* Boulder, Colorado: Westview Press.

Coleman, James S. et al. 1988. *Equality of educational opportunity.* Salem, New Hampshire: Ayer Inc.

Gordon, Edmund G. 1999. *Education and justice: A view from the back of the bus.* New York: Teachers College Press.

Grossman, Herbert. 1998. *Achieving educational equality.* Springfield, Illinois: Charles Thomas.

Helfand, Duke. 2000. Report finds "glaring racial inequalities" in public schools. *Los Angeles Times*, 8 March.

Heubert, Jay P., ed. 1999. *Law and school reform.* New Haven: Yale University Press.

Houston, Paul D. and Schneider, Joe. 1999. Drive by critics and silver bullets. *Phi Delta Kappan*, June.

Howe, Kenneth R. 1997. *Understanding equal educational opportunity.* New York: Teachers College Press.

Kohn, Alfie. 1998. Only for my kid: How privileged parents undermine school reform. *Phi Delta Kappan*, April.

Kozol, Jonathan. 1991. *Savage inequalities.* New York: Crown Publishers, Inc.

Mitchell, Bruce. 1971. *The classroom pursuit of creativity: one strategy that worked. Journal of Research and Development in Education.* Vol. 4, No. 3.

Mitchell, Bruce. 1991. *The ten schools program: A courageous attempt to improve the school performance of inner-city youth.* Urban Education, Vol. 25 No. 4.

National Commission on Children. 1991. *Beyond rhetoric: A new American agenda for children and families.* Washington D.C.: U.S. Government Printing Office.

Persell, Carolyn. 1998. *Education and inequality.* New York: The Free Press.

United States Department of Education. 1998. *State comparisons of education statistics: 1969-70 to 1996-97.* Washington, D.C.: United States Department of Education, National Center for Educational Statistics.

Washington Department of Public Instruction. 1978. *State general report and district level summaries.* Olympia: State Superintendent of Public Instruction.

Zirkel, Perry A. and Richardson, Sharon Nalbone. 1988. *A digest of Supreme Court decisions affecting education.* Bloomington, Indiana: Phi Delta Kappa Educational Foundation.

4

Gifted Education:
An Elitist Practice?

During the second half of the 20th century, gifted education programs became popular in schools and school districts throughout the entire world. In fact, one of the authors conducted a study during the decade of the '80s and reported on the programs in a majority of the participating United Nations countries. Twenty-nine of the responding countries described special programs which were functioning for able learners. Sadly, the developing countries reported that funding problems prevented them from crafting such educational enterprises even though they felt they were necessary.

Nonetheless, the 86 responses made it clear that special programs for able learners was an issue which was being taken seriously throughout the world. However, this study and some of the sociological literature continue to address the charges of elitism in special programs for able learners. Some argue that gifted education programs are little more than elitist in nature since most of the participants come from affluent families. Others argue that gifted/talented education programs are merely attempts to individualize educational programs in that they seek to meet the educational needs of precocious learners who often become bored in the regular classroom because they already have mastered the material for their grade level.

To exacerbate the problems, there seems to be an unfortunate feeling on the part of some parents that to have their children placed in special programs for the talented and gifted elevates their own psyche. In fact one author refers to a concept referred to as "my kid is gifted. . . . and yours isn't." This notion will be discussed later in the chapter. And finally, there are the nagging problems of how to identify bright kids and what should their curriculum be.

GIFTED EDUCATION IN THE UNITED STATES:
A BRIEF HISTORY

The topic of gifted/talented education in the United States is driven by the fascination with human intelligence and what it signifies for educators. One of the first famous pioneers in intelligence measurement in the United States was Louis Terman who conducted his Genetic Studies of Genius at Stanford University in 1921. But although Terman was a key pioneer and largely responsible for the creation of the Stanford Binet Intelligence tests, the earliest roots of the "movement" can actually be traced to the St. Louis plan of 1868 which contained a flexible promotion plan. Elizabeth, New Jersey also pioneered one of the early tracking systems in 1886 and New York City's Rapid Advancement classes were in place as early as 1900.

However, Terman's creation of the early intelligence tests provided American educators with a measurement instrument which made it possible to compare the mental performance of students. Unfortunately, these instruments were flawed from the very beginning. Terman based his concept of measurement largely on the work of Binet who created his instruments for French educators who were trying to do a better job of placing children in the schools. Binet argued that they were not to be considered valid measures of human intelligence since he wasn't sure how to measure it accurately. In spite of such disclaimers, Terman translated the French instruments into English and normed the scores with an audience of European American children from Palo Alto, California. In spite of the early problems and the ensuing arguments over intelligence definitions, the measurement of school children in the United States became popular and by the year 2000 had reached a level of popularity that few educators had even dreamed of.

Unfortunately, another problem affected the study of genius and the corresponding programs for the education of gifted/talented youngsters. Terman was heavily influenced by Sir Francis Galton who did his famous studies in Europe. He came to the conclusion that racial factors influenced human intelligence. He believed that in general, Caucasian persons appeared to exhibit higher levels of intelligence than persons from other racial groups. This belief has had a profound effect on some educators throughout the history of education in the United States, even though subsequent studies have clearly refuted these early beliefs in high intelligence based on racial factors alone.

While there were a number of experimental efforts in developing special programs for gifted/talented students during the first half of the 20th century, the new movement seemed to get underway in earnest during the second 50 years of the century. One of the motivating factors was the 1950 report of the Educational Policies Commission of the National Education Association (NEA) which disclosed that the neglect of mentally superior students was a "social waste." But while this provocative declaration stirred up sentiment for the creation of gifted/talented programs it also motivated criticisms of elitism from some quarters. The argument was that if the country was truly "democratic" it would subscribe to a doctrine of egalitarianism, ensuring that the same human and financial efforts were expended for every American child.

Another important milestone in the evolution of gifted/talented education programs in the United States was the creation of the National Association for Gifted Children (NAGC) in 1954. This organization lobbied for legislation and programs which were specifically tailored to meet the needs of intellectually superior students. The NAGC argued that the special programs should begin as early as possible.

Further motivation for the creation of special programs for able learners surfaced during 1957 when the Russian launching of Sputnik (described in chapter one) increased the pressure for starting special programs which were specially designed for intellectually superior students. However, without a Ministry of Education which prescribed procedures for the country as a whole, the efforts at best were of a piecemeal nature.

Important pioneers in the gifted education "movement" included E. Paul Torrance, who pioneered the development of creative thinking tests which became an important arm of gifted education programs throughout the country. While at the University of Minnesota's Bureau of Educational Research during the '50s and up to the mid-'60s, Torrance created his tests of creativity which were widely used in the identification of students for participation in school programs for the intellectually gifted. Three conferences on gifted/talented issues were held at the University of Minnesota during Torrance's tenure there. Thus, 1959, and 1960 conferences were organized by Torrance and Maynard Reynolds. National educational figures such as Calvin Taylor from the University of Utah and the University of Chicago's J. W. Getzels were some of the prominent participants. These conferences had a highly motivational effect and inspired the development of additional gifted/talented programs throughout the country. Torrance's classic work, *Guiding Creative Talent*, shed important light on the identification and programming issues related to the education of intellectually superior students. The appendix of Torrance's book contains information on administering and scoring his creativity instruments.

At this time in history, other pioneers were studying the personality traits of gifted/talented students. Among the more significant undertakings were the investigations of Getzels and Jackson at the University of Chicago. These studies were conducted with the high school students at the University's Laboratory school. The results revealed that among the numbers of intellectually superior students there were subjects who tended to be either high or low creative thinkers. Interestingly, the higher creative thinkers placed a much stronger value on humor and good mental health than did the low creativity group. Obviously, these critical findings motivated other studies pertaining to the personality traits of intellectually superior students.

But after this spate of interest in gifted/talented education programs, the effort diminished until 1971 when the famous Marland Report was issued. Authored by Commissioner of the Department of Education Sidney Marland, the report was presented the U. S. Congress. Key consultants to Marland were Catherine Bruch, Louis Fliegler, Joseph Renzulli, Irving Sato, Ruth Martinson, Jacob Getzels, and

A. Harry Passow. It contained a definition of giftedness, and identified six differ-ent kinds of giftedness. It also posited that between three and five percent of the population should be thought of as being gifted. The impetus from the Marland Report led to the establishment of the Office of Gifted and Talented in the Depart-ment of Education. This occurred just prior to the establishment of the position of secretary of education, a cabinet position, during the presidency of Jimmy Carter.

During the same period of time Irving Sato established the National/State Leadership Institute on the Gifted and Talented, (N/S-LTI-G/T) an arm of Dr. James Cowan's Ventura County Superintendent of Schools' office. Utilizing such consultants as Robert Ponce, E. Paul Torrance, John Gowan, Joseph Renzulli, Dorothy Sisk, Mary Frasier, Catherine Bruch, James J. Gallagher, Mary Meeker, Bruce Mitchell, and Ed Dodson, the purpose of the conferences was to assist states and school districts in the creation and sustenance of educational programs for the gifted and talented.

THE EARLY CONCERNS OF ELITISM IN
PROGRAMS FOR THE GIFTED

After the 1954 *Brown v. Board of Education* Supreme Court decision the Amer-ican Civil Rights Movement addressed a number of key American problems in regard to the glaring racial inequalities following the termination of the Civil War in 1865. Due to the racist practices of school segregation, Jim Crow laws, redlin-ing, sundown laws and the like, African Americans and other minorities were forced to deal with numerous inequities, many of them being directly related to educational practices. The nation dealt with the most glaring problems first. Con-sequently, the problem of subtle racist practices in the schools were not addressed until later. The issue of who gets to participate in gifted/talented programs was not addressed vigorously until the decade of the '70s.

Irving Sato, N/S-LTI-G/T director, organized the first national conference on the "disadvantaged gifted." The conference attempted to address the needs of the glaring under-representation of African American, Native American, and Latino children in school programs for the talented and gifted. In virtually every pro-gram for able learners there was a glaring over-representation of European-American children. One of the authors visited a gifted/talented school program in the Yakima Valley in Washington state in the late '70s. He discovered that in the school attendance area European American children consisted of only about 40 percent of the total school population. Yet, when he visited the school district's gifted/talented education program, ALL the students were European Americans.

On another visit to a school where he conducted a program for low-income Latino children in the Los Angeles Harbor area, he discovered that in an elementary school with a student population of 1,100 children, only two had been selected for partic-ipation in California's Gifted and Talented Education (GATE) program! If the stan-dard three percent of the population had been considered to be "gifted" there should have been about 33 children in the school who should have been participating in the district's GATE program.These inequities existed throughout the country.

N/S-LTI-G/T PROGRAM TOPICS

A 1973 conference organized by the N/S-LTI-G/T featured speakers who addressed 19 different topics related to the education of bright low-income students and children of color. To cite a few examples of the concerns addressed by leading gifted/talented educators throughout the nation, Alexinia Baldwin described a program she helped develop in the Birmingham, Alabama schools. It consisted of a special educational offering for gifted African American students. These students were examples of the young persons who were not chosen to participate in gifted/talented education programs because their test scores were sometimes lower than those of their European American counterparts.

The African American students in the Birmingham program experienced an intellectual growth spurt during their first year of participation. However, the author felt that this spurt was probably due to a "Hawthorne Effect." However, the Hawthorne Effect continued into the second year and the programs were deemed to be highly successful.

Steven Moreno described the identification procedures to be a "myth" for Latino students. He cited statistics which revealed that Latino children were woefully under-represented in school programs. Interestingly, he prepared an alternative identification procedure which relied on special selection criterion including rating on such traits as creativity, reasoning, and problem-solving skills.

In addition, Moreno recommended that educators use such factors as social effectiveness, motivation, self-confidence, and competitiveness in the identification process for Latino gifted/talented children. He argued that bilingual language factors made it difficult for Latino children to pass the required tests for admission to programs for the talented and gifted.

Dorothy Sisk, the first national director of gifted/talented education, faulted the measurement instruments used in identifying participants for gifted/talented education programs. She believed that these tests measured only a bare minimum of the thinking behaviors that were indicative of superior intelligence. She argued that such factors as alertness, curiosity, verbal ability, aggressive abstract thinking, and self assurance were the behaviors that most teachers felt were more accurate indicators of high intelligence than the test scores per se.

Other contributors described alternative ways of identifying students who were not particularly good at responding to standard measurement devices, while other experts identified program modules which would meet the needs of low-income students who tended to respond poorly to the kinds of strategies which worked well for European-American students who came from affluent families.

EQUAL EDUCATIONAL OPPORTUNITIES AND
GIFTED EDUCATION

The notion of equality historically has been a fundamental cornerstone of many U.S. institutions, particularly in the field of education. Equality of opportunity has generally related to the issue of creating "a level playing field" in order for all students to be able to compete equally in the schoolroom. The schools have attempted to provide special services for children needing special assistance due to various handicaps (physical, emotional, psychological, intellectual, etc.). The inclusion of special programs for intellectually precocious students has often been viewed as an extension of that concept. That is, unusually bright children are entitled to specially crafted programs in order to ensure that the curriculum and instruction is appropriate for them.

Another rationale for the inclusion of programs for able learners has been related to the notion that students have very individualized needs. Some are capable of learning faster than others, while some are able to learn much more than others. Therefore, in order to meet the educational needs of everyone, it is necessary to find ways of individualizing the curriculum and instruction in order to meet these needs. Consequently, special programs for able learners are appropriate because they must be intellectually challenged and to do so requires them to interact with each other in order to improve their academic prowess. After all, the argument continues, we do that for talented musicians in band and orchestra and we also do that for talented athletes in sports programs.

Educators have always wanted to challenge students to their fullest in order to maximize learning. Tennis players do not improve much when they only play opponents who are beneath their level and in a like manner, intellectually superior students often do not reach their fullest potential unless they can interact with others who are capable of thinking at a high level. Unfortunately, to say that publicly automatically conjures up images of elitism, encouraging remarks such as "Oh those gifted kids think they're so smart." And since there is a high correlation between per capita income and school performance, a connection is sometimes made between intellectual snobbery and affluence. Yet another common notion is that if children are so smart, why do they need special programs? After all, there aren't any special programs for "nearly able" learners or "slightly unable" learners, so what's the big deal about being gifted?

The concerns about charges of elitism in connection with gifted/talented programs have caused educators to explore strategies for involving more students in programs for able learners. One successful venture has been the University of Connecticut's Joseph Renzulli's ideas on his so-called "revolving door" program. This model utilizes approaches which allow bright students with a particular aptitude to participate in special programs for shorter periods of time. After their revolving door term is up, they go back to the regular classroom and other able learners participate. In this manner a larger number of students are able to become involved in so-called "gifted education programs."

DO WEIGHTED GRADES CONTRIBUTE TO
THE ELITISM CHARGES?

Another problem connected with programs for the gifted and talented students has surfaced during the middle school and high school years. Able learners have often been placed in honors programs or other "advanced-placement" enterprises. Of course in a highly competitive country such as the United States, letter grades have been a major concern for students, parents, and teachers. If the competition for grades becomes too keen, some students may wish to opt out of such educational ventures since grade point averages (GPAs) are becoming even more important in determining which students should be admitted to schools such as Harvard, Massachusetts Institute of Technology, University of Chicago, Yale, Stanford, Princeton, California Institute of Technology, and a host of other outstanding American institutions of higher education.

If the competition for high grades becomes too great, some students have been known to shy away from high-competition classes in which mostly the brightest students are enrolled. The thinking is that it would be a lot easier getting a high GPA if you didn't have to compete against the brightest kids in the school all the time. So in order to lure intellectually precocious students into special honors programs and the like, "weighted grades" have sometimes been used as an educational ploy which might encourage them to participate against other extremely bright students

Unfortunately, that also backfires sometimes. Other students sometimes feel that they worked at least as hard as the "able learners" and they resent the fact that their grades count less then their "gifted/talented" counterparts. And although the authors know of no court cases challenging the constitutionality of such a practice, it would seem that the use of weighted grades might come into conflict with the equal protection clause of the Fourteenth Amendment of the Constitution.

Recently, one of the authors conducted a small pilot study of both private and public colleges and universities and found that as a general rule, weighted grades did not seem to be taken seriously. Yet, the practice persists in middle schools and high schools and many parents of talented and gifted children fight to maintain the weighted grade practice. Unfortunately, this practice tends to perpetuate the charges of elitism in programs for able learners.

THE NATURE OF EQUALITY

In the United States, the notion of equality has always been a prominent concept in terms of constitutional guarantees as articulated in the U.S. Constitution. Unfortunately, legal definitions of the term have not been clearly established, particularly as the word relates to the equal rights amendments that many states have added to their constitutions. And while numerous written doctrines in the United States have consistently argued for equality and equal applications practices, inequalities still persist. Indeed, Jonathan Kozol's book, *Savage Inequalities*, pointed out many of the grossly inequitable practices in the field of education.

Other nations, such as Norway and Sweden, have historically attempted to rely on egalitarianism principles in their education systems. Indeed, in the 1987 international gifted education study conducted by one of the authors, neither country had special programs for the gifted and talented, a common response among the

Scandinavian countries. Indeed, the Netherlands opined that more harm than good would come from such practices.

Yet, other countries, particularly the United States and Japan, have crafted strong programs for able learners, believing that it was necessary to ensure that the best minds in the nation were not wasted. In fact, the educational system in both countries has contained elements of elitism with the best educational offerings being available to students from privileged groups. Because of its emphasis on capitalistic principles, the best education available to American school children is often provided to the most wealthy. Indeed, the funding inequalities articulated elsewhere in this book are well documented.

The egalitarian ideals of de Tocqueville, Mills, and Locke are only concepts developed in writing and speech until they are exemplified in actual practice. To illustrate the difficulty in applying the principle of equality, let us examine the case of Alan Bakke, who sought a career change and applied to the University of California in order to attend medical school. Bakke had already applied to several universities for entry into their medical schools and he had been turned down in all of them. This occurred at a time in history when California (along with many others) had adapted "affirmative action programs" which attempted to atone for years of discrimination against women and minorities who had not been admitted to such august educational undertakings. Affirmative action programs were designed in order to ensure that incoming medical school classes would more closely approximate the gender, race, ethnic, and income levels of the society at large. Prior to that time, the medical profession was dominated by affluent European American males. Universities such as the University of California-Davis, set aside "quota slots" for women and minorities in order to make up for these unequal practices of the past. Often, these quotas consisted of about 10 percent of the total number of entry slots.

After Bakke was rejected at the University of California-Davis, he decided to sue the university on the grounds of "reverse discrimination." In other words, Bakke, a European American male, argued that his constitutional rights had been violated and the university refused to allow him to reapply for admission through the "quota pool." The U.S. Supreme Court overturned a California Supreme Court decision, ruling that the university's action in disallowing Bakke to be reconsidered in the quota pool was unconstitutional. However, they ruled that such practices were constitutionally acceptable as long as the institution did not prevent candidates such as Bakke from being reconsidered in the quota pool. In other words, nobody could be excluded from the quota pool on the basis of gender, race, or ethnicity. The institution can use any criteria they wish as long as the original non-selected candidates are allowed to be reconsidered if they so wish. In other words, the attempts to make up for past discrimination cannot be rectified through the use of new discriminatory practices.

Thus, it can be seen that the ideas about equality and equality for whom are very complicated issues. Quite often in American schools it has meant that equality of educational opportunity has been accessible only to the more affluent. To be sure, the lack of education for Native Americans until more recent times; the refusal to educate the children of slaves and the pitiful segregated schools for African American children after slavery; the woefully inadequate schools for children from poverty pockets such as Appalachia; and the segregated schools for migrant farm workers have given the nation a black eye. And given the United States' red-hot economy and the burgeoning number of millionaires, it would appear that "equality" might be in danger of becoming the province of only the more affluent classes.

IDENTIFICATION OF GIFTED CHILDREN

The identification of children for participation in gifted/talented education programs has presented an enormous problem for educators. Some of the more basic arguments relate to the definition of intelligence. The very best tests of intelligence measure about six different thinking behaviors. Yet the more sophisticated models of intelligence developed by such researchers as J.P. Guilford in his model of multiple factored intelligence (Structure of the Intellect Model), have identified 120 different intelligences. Many of these thinking behaviors are not measured in some of the intelligence tests used to identify children for able learner programs.

However, in an attempt to compensate for this difficulty in defining intelligence, some school districts have used carefully developed behavioral models such as Joseph Renzulli's excellent behavioral checklist which lists a number of learning characteristics pertaining to creative thinking, leadership, motivation, etc. Each behavioral trait is scored through the use of a four-point Likert scale and the total points are tallied.

Other school districts utilize the Torrance Tests of Creativity (TTCs) in order to acquire an accurate measure of the student's ability to engage in synthesis tasks which require the development of unique ideas and creative solutions to problems. In an attempt to identify children from non-European American backgrounds, a few school districts have utilized other measurement devices such as the DeAvila Cartoon Conservation Series. These and numerous other strategies have been adopted in order to ensure fairness in the selection process.

However, in spite of all these efforts, the fact remains that in the final analysis, it is often difficult to answer the question "What makes one able learner eligible for the special programs while the next one was rejected?" Educators are often hard pressed to provide cogent answers to that question. Therefore, some school districts have opted for strategies that are inclusive rather than exclusive. One example is the Schoolwide Enrichment Model (SEM), developed by Joseph Renzulli and utilized in Hartford, Connecticut.

Part of the philosophy of the program is that rather than using I.Q. scores for the permanent placement of students in programs for the gifted, perhaps the emphasis should be on talent development instead. This research-supported plan emphasizes using the existing school structure to infuse more effective practices into school programs in order to increase student effort, enjoyment, and performance. Rather than relegating the acquisition of higher-level thinking skills to only the top 2 or 3 percent of the students, these skills are pursued by all students. It is thought that strategies such as this can help diffuse the charges of elitism which plague the profession.

GIFTED EDUCATION:
THE PROVINCE OF PRIVILEGED PARENTS?

Historically, states and school districts which have not originally been "gifted program friendly" have sometimes been forced to initiate such programs for able learners because of the clout of affluent parents who have fought to acquire the best education possible for their children. If the parents are convinced that their children are unusually bright (and they often are) they have used their influence to coax and cajole school districts into creating appropriate programs for able learners. But often elitism indeed rears its ugly head.

Alfie Kohn, a writer and lecturer on education and human behavior has argued that wealthy parents are willing to sacrifice other children in favor of their own. Moreover, he has stated that from Amherst to Palo Alto, highly educated European American parents have called for school programs which have effectively kept children of color out of accelerated programs for able learners. Specifically, he has complained about a European American constituency which has lobbied fiercely for a "skill and drill" approach to mathematics, contrary to the National Council of Mathematics Teachers (NCMT) conceptual learnings standards.

The same author lamented the fact that an attempt to provide underachieving San Diego students with a support system which would enable them to achieve in higher-level courses ran into stiff resistance from some of the city's affluent European American parents. And in an affluent Buffalo suburb, parents of honor students fought an attempt to replace highly competitive letter grades with meaningful reports based on the achievement of behavioral standards. Jeannie Oakes, author of *Keeping Track* referred to such groups as the *Volvo Vigilantes*. They are mostly affluent, outspoken European Americans who know how to make the laws work to their advantage. A good percentage of their children are high performers, many of whom are in honors and/or advanced placement classes or classes for the gifted and talented. And while they may be pro-choice rather than anti-choice and speak despairingly of Pat Robertson, Jessie Helms or Rush Limbaugh, they generally seem to be allied with the far right on educational issues.

Harvey Daniels of National Louis University has even argued that it seems that a great deal of the fuss is clearly about winning and losing. He stated that it seems as if it's not enough for their kids to win, there also must be losers. Of course, that may not be surprising, given the infatuation for aggressive competition that grips the country now. Even a five-year-old child, Jon Benet Ramsey, was involved in beauty competition before her murder.

And while the early notions about American education stressed the need for Americans to become well-educated, responsible members of a democratic voting society, the emphasis seems to have become extraordinarily self-centered. Parents who represent vocal groups of European American children often seem to have become disciples of the "what's in it for my kid and to hell with yours" philosophy.

CURRENT EFFORTS TO IDENTIFY
BRIGHT LOW-INCOME CHILDREN

Earlier in the chapter, we discussed the efforts of the N/S-LTI-G/T to identify children of color and low-income children for participation in special programs for able learners. In order to assess the current status, one of the authors conducted a pilot study of the school districts in Washington State. Just one question was asked in a brief survey instrument: "Do you employ a special procedure for ensuring that children from poverty backgrounds and/or children of color are included in your district's gifted/talented program?" The responders were asked to check "yes" or "no." If they checked "yes" they were requested to supply a description of the procedure.

Just 31 of the 158 responding school districts replied that they utilized special procedures which would include under-represented students in their district's special programs for the gifted/talented. However, 11 of the program descriptions were clearly lacking in overt attempts to ensure the inclusion of such children in special programs for able learners. The remaining program descriptions included strategies such as "targeted marketing" which relies on the identification of all the district's children of color who score high on achievement tests; and the inclusion of 26 percent of the eligible participant pool for further screening, thus increasing the odds of including low-income/children of color candidates for final selection.

While these strategies seem to have excellent potential, it should be noted that just 20 out of the 158 responding school districts seemed to have viable identification procedures which would include this particular audience of students in gifted and talented programs. That represents just 13 percent of the responding school districts which seems to indicate that this is not presently a major concern of Washington educators. Sadly, it is quite likely that the other 49 states operate in a similar fashion.

REFERENCES

Backrach, Peter. 1967. *The theory of democratic elitism: A critique*. Boston: Little, Brown & Co.

Baldwin, Alexinia. 1975. Identifying the disadvantaged. *The National Conference on the Disadvantaged Gifted*. Ventura, California: Ventura County Superintendent of Schools.

Bottomore, T. B. 1964. *Elites and society*. New York: Basic Books.

Clark, Barbara. 1992. *Growing up gifted*. Columbus: Macmillan.

Fitzgerald, Ellen A. 1975. *The first national conference on the disadvantaged gifted.* Ventura, California: Ventura County Superintendent of Schools.

Gallagher, James J, and Gallagher, Shelagh. 1974. *Teaching the gifted child.* Boston: Allyn & Bacon.

Galton, Francis. 1869. *Hereditary genius: An inquiry into its law and consequences.* London: Macmillan & Company.

Guilford, J.P. 1977. *Way beyond the I.Q.* Buffalo: Creative Education Foundation.

Kohl, Alfie. 1998. Only for my kid. *Phi Delta Kappan,* Vol. 79, No. 8, pp. 568-577.

Millar, Garnet W. 1995. *The creativity man.* Norwood, New Jersey: Ablex Publishing Co.

Mitchell, Bruce. 1999. *Does anyone care about bright "at-risk" kids anymore?* Spokane: Unpublished Paper.

Mitchell, Bruce and Williams, William. 1989. *From Afghanistan to Zimbabwe: gifted education efforts in the world community.* New York: Peter Lang.

Moreno, Steven. 1975. *The first national conference on the disadvantaged gifted.* Ventura California: Ventura County Superintendent of Schools.

Piirto, Jane. 1994. *Talented children and adults: Their development and education.* New York: Merrill.

Rae, Douglas. 1981. *Equalities.* Cambridge: Harvard University Press.

Renzulli, Joseph S. 1998. A rising tide lifts all ships: Developing the gifts of all students. *Phi Delta Kappan*, Vol. 80, No. 2, pp. 1-4.

Shurkin, Joel N. 1992. *Terman's kids.* Boston: Little, Brown & Company.

Sisk, Dorothy. 1975. Developing teacher mediators/teacher training for the disadvantaged gifted. *The First National Conference on the Disadvantaged Gifted.* Ventura, California: Ventura County Superintendent of Schools.

Terman, Louis M. et al. 1925, 1926, 1930, 1947, 1949. *Genetic studies of genius.* Stanford, California: Stanford University Press.

Torrance, E. Paul. 1962. *Guiding creative talent.* Englewood Cliffs, New Jersey: Prentice-Hall Inc.

Ventura County Superintendent of Schools. 1978. *Advantage: Disadvantaged gifted.* Ventura, California: Ventura County Superintendent of Schools.

5

Multicultural Education: An Antidote to Educational Inequality?

After the American Civil Rights Movement, educators searched for ways to utilize many of the ideas which had become rallying cries for those involved in the movement. Until the '60s, the schools had subscribed to a Eurocentric approach to American history and numerous racist practices had helped to define American education. Indeed, many non-European American students sometimes felt inferior because their various microcultures were not dealt with accurately in the school curriculum. For example, American history books often started with the arrival of Columbus, virtually ignoring the rich pre-Columbian history that had existed for thousands of years prior to the arrival of the Europeans.

Consequently, multicultural education efforts attempt to address America's racial and cultural diversity as if it were the nation's most valuable natural resource. Instead of painting inaccurate pictures of the contributions of the country's microcultures, multicultural education efforts are designed to help young children acquire positive values about the burgeoning cultural and racial diversity which enriches the country.

But, multicultural education is more than appreciating racial and ethnic diversity. It's also about the equality of opportunity guaranteed by the nation's Constitution. It's about gender equity and ensuring that young women have the same kinds of opportunities in the economic marketplace as young men. It's about demanding that the most poverty-stricken student in the country has the same probability of enrolling in CalTech or Harvard as the wealthiest son or daughter of the nation's richest family. And perhaps most importantly, it's also about helping children learn to love and appreciate people who are different, rather than harboring feelings of suspicion or even out-and-out hatred.

In regard to hatred, the nation has been experiencing a frightening increase in hate crimes, such as the murder of a California mail carrier who was of a different race than his assassin, an ex-member of the Aryan Nations "church," who murdered him simply because he was not a European American. Neo-Nazi/Skinhead groups have taught their members to hate Jews, African Americans, and nearly everyone who is not of European American heritage. Indeed, the rest of the world is watching and wondering what possesses so many members of the American macroculture to harbor such hatred.

Since much of these negative attitudes are learned at home, children must be exposed to multicultural educational programs in the schools if they are to have a chance at a fulfilled life as opposed to a life of hatred and doubts about their ultimate worth as human beings. It's a tall order for schools, but multicultural education approaches might be able to turn around the lives of some children who could easily become the foils of Grand Dragons and other hate group leaders.

WHAT ARE MULTICULTURAL EDUCATION PROGRAMS?

This is a difficult question to answer. Every author has a pet definition for this concept. However, for this chapter, "multicultural education" is viewed as consisting of five basic premises pertaining to positive human interaction, particularly as it should occur in a pluralistic macroculture like the one that exists in the United States:

1. Just as money is the basic unit for the economist, culture is the unit of analysis for the mature, sensitive teacher.
2. Education in a free society like America requires teachers to respect the rights of students to be culturally different.
3. Education for cultural pluralism requires the rejection of assimilationist dogma.
4. Multicultural education requires the maintenance of native languages and cultural value systems.
5. Multicultural education promotes the development of tolerance, respect and appreciation of differences in human beings.
6. Multicultural education reflects the normal human experience.

The goal of multicultural educators should be twofold: first, it is necessary to help all students realize that their cultural heritage has value. However, the second goal is equally important because teachers must also help students realize that other microcultures are equally valuable. Members of different cultures are important human beings simply because they are alive.

In keeping with this philosophy, some multicultural education practitioners have articulated a concept that is of critical importance. It is referred to as the "salad theory" or "stew theory" and is perceived as an alternative to the old "melting pot theory" originated by Israel Zangwill, a New York playwright. The stew or salad theory posits that human beings have the potential to provide the same kind of excitement as the stew or salad. Each ingredient adds to the total flavor. Subtract the tomatoes in the salad and the total entity is not as tasty just as the clam chowder suffers if the cook forgets to include the clams! Likewise, human interaction is more interesting and more palatable if people are able to interact with folks who are different.

In order to help students become more aware of their own levels of multicultural functioning, it is sometimes useful to identify a number of differing levels of multicultural functioning. A useful model was first developed by James Banks from the University of Washington and this work is an adaptation of his ideas.

Level One is *Cultural Rejection.* This is the most damaging stage of multicultural functioning because people possess negative feelings about their own culture. These attitudes often result in inadequate self-concepts which could make any kind of learning extremely difficult. Sometimes this level might describe an entire microculture.

Level Two is referred to as *Cultural Encapsulation.* At this point, people for the first time have become able to accept their own microculture and they may acquire an intense pride in it. However, they may also reject the value of any other group. Because they feel so strongly about their own microculture, they may become dangerously ethnocentric. They may feel that their microculture is the only one that matters and all others are inferior. But even though level-two persons may even become members of highly racist groups, it is still a necessary stage, since it is the first stage of acceptance, although at an irrational level.

Level Three is more positive, since it is a learning stage. This stage of *Bicultural Preparation* is the level at which the person becomes interested in another microculture. While the individual is still harboring some of the old ethnocentric beliefs, the attitudes and values in the person's native microculture are becoming refined while at the same time an interest in a second microculture is developing. All of a sudden the other microculture is being perceived as something that might be of value.

Level Four is referred to as *Cultural Bilingualism.* This is an important stage of multicultural development since the learners have now fully accepted a second microculture on an equal level as their own. The old loyalty to the person's original microcultural still exists, but the second one is of equal importance. At this fourth stage, the people can function in the other culture as comfortably as they can in their own.

Level Five is called *Polycultural Functioning.* Here, people enjoy interacting with persons from a wide variety of different microcultures. Instead of merely tolerating human differences, they seek out pluralistic interactions because they are more exciting and fulfilling. They become knowledgeable about a variety of microcultures and prefer to seek out relationships with culturally different people.

Level Six is referred to as *International Citizenship.* At this point, people have actually become **Citizens of the World.** Culturally different groups of people all over the world are viewed as being unique and interesting. The person can interact with anyone from any world culture with equal comfort and enjoyment.

FRIENDS AND FOES OF MULTICULTURAL EDUCATION

While most educators are staunch advocates of the notion of multicultural education, there are also some enemies. Among the foes of this concept are those who would prefer a Eurocentric spin on educational practices in the United States along with the so-called religious right of the Republican Party. Along with their agendas of prayer in school, teaching conservative Christian values, and a strict Eurocentric approach to history and the social sciences, this group has listed multicultural education as one of the items on its "hit list."

These and other foes of multicultural education often believe that the problems are so severe that children should be taken out of the public schools and either be placed in private schools or home schooled. Members of such right-leaning organizations as Exodus 2000, Rescue 2010 and the Separation of School and State Alliance are convinced that the public schools are immoral because of their secular nature. However, secularism in education is based on the establishment clause of the First Amendment which requires the separation of church and state. This means that because of the nation's Constitution, the public schools must remain secular and refrain from promoting any religious views.

Ironically, many of the outspoken critics of multicultural education seem to embrace the teaching of the exceptional and culturally different, but at the same time seem to reject multicultural education programs, arguing instead for some vague and nebulous type of assimilation into a mysterious "common culture" which nobody can seem to agree on. Presumably it has something to do with English Americans and a poorly defined macroculture. Indeed, some critics such as Ravitch have worried that multicultural education programs might possibly cause the country to become dis-united in some similar manner as the Soviet Union. She has wondered if multicultural education advocates were actually extremists who encouraged American microcultures to pull away from an ill-defined "national ideal."

But other critics have argued against multicultural education from a human relations perspective. These critics argue that little attention is paid to the importance of love and interpersonal caring. Many in these groups feel that multicultural education efforts are misguided when they emphasize the acquisition of cognitive information about American microcultures as opposed to the exploration of interpersonal feelings and social issues of power which affect the relationships between different American microcultures. While these two groups do not harbor antagonistic feelings about each other, they tend to move in different directions.

It appears to the authors that these two areas of concern are not mutually exclusive. Rather, the argument could be made that either position without the other might eventually result in multicultural education programs becoming totally ineffective. Cognitively, people need to understand the history, concerns, and character of different microcultures. Obviously, not to examine such information affectively does not allow the learner to fully grasp the complexities of microcultures which differ from their own. Strategies must be developed by educators which require students to "walk in the other person's moccasins" before making judgments.

OTHER PROBLEMS WITH MULTICULTURAL
EDUCATION PROGRAMS

Another criticism of multicultural education has come from some microcultures which were being studied in order for multicultural education students to acquire a better understanding of people who are different from themselves. Some groups have claimed that they have received short shrift compared to other microcultures. For example, African Americans, Latinos, and European American women have received a great deal of attention in multicultural studies. However, the Hmong of Southeast Asia, a small American microculture, have not. Neither have Puerto Ricans or Basques because of their small numbers. So multicultural education educators have been hard pressed to provide equal time to all groups. While it can be safely said that nobody intentionally wishes to omit any particular group from multicultural studies, time usually prevents instructors from spending equal time on each American microculture.

To compound the problem, some groups may not wish to be included in stud ies of multicultural education. Because all cultures have heterogeneous thinkers in their midst, some people simply wish to assimilate in the American "melting pot" and aren't interested in maintaining some of their cultural traditions. Moreover, since most Americans have not received an effective multicultural education approach in their own schooling, it is sometimes difficult to envision the most effective ways of utilizing such approaches. Moreover, to do an adequate job of developing empathetic understandings of American microcultures, educators must have a great depth of cultural knowledge.

For example, in understanding the problems encountered by African Americans, it is necessary to have an understanding of the economic, geographical, historical, and racist roots of slavery. Educators need to know something about the cultural traditions of West Africans. For example, the Ghanaian talking drum was used first to communicate in Africa and later to communicate problems which existed on the American plantations. Also, in order to understand the West African contributions to the development of American jazz, it is necessary to understand the racist, economic and cultural problems which afflicted African Americans in the United States. Without understanding what motivated the development of the minstrel show, the blues, and American jazz, it is probably impossible for educators to understand the microculture of African American people.

In a like manner, in order to develop a cognitive/affective appreciation for Native Americans, the teacher must know what motivated the Europeans to come to the "new world" and what damage their notion of "manifest destiny" did to the Native American macroculture. Their lust for riches and a "better" life than they had in Europe provided a high level of motivation. But in addition to this knowledge, a good multicultural educator must also be familiar with the nature of treaties between the various tribes and the new European American governments as well as the cultural conflicts which affect both groups. Historically, the Cherokee Trail of Tears, motivated by the Removal Act of 1830 during the administration of President Andrew Jackson, is a complicated issue involving racism, economics, and concerns about the safety of European American settlers. This and other similar actions would change the way of life for many Native Americans forever and teachers must understand the implications of such historical actions in order for students to come to grips with a multitude of complicated multicultural actions.

STATE EFFORTS IN MULTICULTURAL EDUCATION

Iowa and New Mexico have two of the better multicultural education programs in the United States. New Mexico has a planned multicultural education program which is headed by the director of the Bilingual Multicultural Education Program. New Mexico provides leadership for school districts which need assistance in developing their programs. Assistance provided includes workshops, state institutes, research dissemination training institutes, school programs and teacher exchanges.

Since 1989, New Mexico has required teachers to master a number of competencies in the area of bilingual multicultural education. These competencies were approved by the New Mexico State Board of Education. The curriculum stresses cultural pluralism as opposed to an assimilationist philosophy. Also, New Mexico has special programs for teaching children in their native language in order to facilitate learning.

New Mexico has exhibited a commitment to bilingual multicultural instruction since it achieved statehood in 1912. Moreover, the state's 1912 Constitution still contains provisions which protect the right of all citizens to vote, hold office, or sit on juries regardless of their religion, race, language, or color. The state also has a strict prohibition against school segregation.

In order to provide equal educational opportunities for all children, New Mexico schools are required to prepare an Educational Plan for Student Success (EPSS) which is a blueprint for ensuring that each New Mexico student will receive an equal education in grades k-12. The plan must be systematically detailed and contain specific strategies for achieving individual success. Descriptions of how student assessment will be carried out must also be included.

The Iowa Code (Chapter 256.11) mandates that the state board shall . . . "promulgate rules to require that a multicultural, nonsexist approach is used in schools and school districts. The education program shall be taught from a multicultural, nonsexist approach." Part of the Iowa Code requirements also mandate a written plan which must be updated every five years. Iowa's state office provides school districts with publications, workshops, and also conducts monitoring services in order to ensure that each local district complies with the multicultural education requirements.

In order to receive their certification, prospective teachers are required to participate in a human relations class that emphasizes multicultural education issues and the school curriculum in Iowa, like New Mexico, emphasizes cultural pluralism as opposed to an assimilationist approach.

While the approaches to pluralism by these two states are applaudable, other states have been slow to develop viable programs for multicultural education efforts. In some cases, the reluctance is politically motivated by right-wing groups as well as the religious right. Consequently, it is safe to say that in the United States there are 50 separate programs which relate to the collective state efforts in multicultural education.

Since education is only a federal interest in the United States, the Department of Education has not mandated specific programs in multicultural education, even though that body has often provided special funding for programs which have some of the elements of multicultural education. For example, in the past, special funds have been allocated for school desegregation, Head Start, and bilingual education, all of which relate to the total package of multicultural education efforts. Unfortunately, the authors' earlier multicultural education study revealed that some states, such as Texas, had no multicultural education program, nobody was in charge of such enterprises, no state funds were utilized, and no leadership in multicultural education existed.

VOICES FOR AND AGAINST MULTICULTURAL EDUCATION

While critics of multicultural education such as Hirsch, Glazer, Ravitch, and Broudy have argued against the utilization of multicultural education, educational scholars such as Banks, Sleeter, Takaki, Gollnick, Chinn, and this book's authors strongly disagree. Hirsch has argued in favor of an inadequately defined "American" culture and linguistic standard. He has expressed a concern that to become immersed in multicultural education efforts could somehow cause the United States to become fragmented and fall apart like the former Soviet Union. However, such pronouncements, often coming from the political and religious rights, miss the total point of multicultural education, which is to bring people together!

In fact, Banks and other advocates of multicultural education have posited that as humans become more educated about and more involved with people who are racially and culturally different from themselves, they become more tolerant of and more interested in human diversity. In fact, some organizations such as the Poverty Law Center of Montgomery, Alabama, has created excellent educational materials which are designed to help teachers develop tolerant attitudes toward persons who are different from themselves.

Indeed, history has revealed the damages that can be attributed to the multitude of racist attitudes which have led to the persecution of microcultures in the United States and the rest of the world as well. Assimilation simply means that all microcultures throughout the world should give up their language and traditions, and acquire those of the ruling group. On the other hand, multicultural education efforts are designed to help students look upon the nation's cultural diversity as the strongest natural resource the country possesses.

Indeed, to rob a group of people of their language, values, religion, and traditions not only deprives a country of its greatest national resource, but presents a barrier to the acquisition of a strong liberal education. To counter that possibility, many efforts are currently underway by Native American groups to maintain their written and spoken languages. Such undertakings obviously strengthen a diverse group of people as long as the efforts are designed to help people achieve the top two levels of multicultural functioning as described earlier in this chapter. Moreover, the United States is one of the few nations around the world that has such a small population of people who are bilingual, trilingual, or multilingual.

Elitism is another enemy of multicultural education. Unfortunately, the enormous drive for affluence in America has caused immeasurable problems for multicultural education. Attempts to curb racist and sexist attitudes rarely command the incomes available to those who are in business/technology/marketing enterprises. Moreover, people who are afflicted by the present drive for wealth and power often care little about equity, racial harmony and the like. The profit motive that is so powerful in business education endeavors is nearly absent in education circles. Consequently, the multicultural education efforts in states such as Iowa and New Mexico are highly encouraging.

WHAT THE SCHOOLS CAN DO

Multicultural education programs can be established in the schools without creating many changes. It all starts with teacher education and an interest by teachers to include multicultural education strands throughout their lesson plans. Many states, such as Washington, now require prospective teachers to receive appropriate exposure to multicultural education philosophy as well as acquiring purposeful and usable multicultural teaching strategies. Moreover, a growing number of university teacher preparation programs require prospective teachers to acquire experiences in working with young people whose culture is different from their own.

In the classroom, teachers can use pluralistic approaches in their teaching as described earlier in this chapter. Teaching tolerance toward all racial and ethnic groups is an absolute necessity. An excellent resource for teachers are the Teaching Tolerance materials which are available from the Southern Poverty Law Center, 400 Washington Avenue, Montgomery, Alabama, 36104.

Revisionist history is also of critical importance. During earlier times, most American history books were written as if the history of the United States somehow commenced with the arrival of Columbus! The idea that Columbus somehow "discovered" the United States is, of course, fallacious. The Anasazi were constructing high-rise apartment buildings in places like Chaco Canyon hundreds of years before the voyages of Columbus and anthropologists have recently made discoveries that place Native Americans within the present-day boundaries of the United States thousands of years before that time. The history curriculum also must deal with the conditions surrounding the arrival of such microcultures as Irish Americans (Potato Famine), African Americans (slavery), English Americans (disenchantment with sovereignty, religious persecution, and economic enhancement), Latinos and Chinese (cheap labor exploitation), eastern Europeans (economic enhancement and freedom), and the Hmong (safety from the victorious North Vietnamese). Obviously, the list could go on and on but these are some examples of what should be included in an honest attempt to deal accurately with American history.

As stated previously, music is the universal language and multicultural education experts argue that music and art can be useful allies to serious multicultural educators.

As discussed earlier, American jazz can become an antidote to racism, even though the art form has suffered from racist practices throughout its history. For example, renown musicians such as Louis Armstrong, sometimes were not allowed to stay where they were playing because of their race! And the early jazz reed player, Sidney Bechet, preferred playing in France because the country was more tolerant of African Americans compared to the United States.

Schools love holidays, and the number of racial and ethnic holidays is enormous. Schools celebrate such special days as Kwanzaa, Cinco de Mayo, Hanukkah, and many others in addition to the more common holidays with European or American origins. These can become part of the multicultural curriculum.

Of great importance to multicultural education programs are the types of displays students see in the halls, classrooms, and elsewhere in the schools. If they see American people from a great variety of racial and cultural backgrounds, they receive important messages about the value of diversity. This can be done with only minimal planning. However, if the pictures they see on a regular basis are pictures of people from the same racial background, they receive another kind of message.

The goals of school districts and individual schools are also important. Equal opportunity must not only be articulated verbally, but carried out in practice. For example, children from the culture of poverty simply do not have equal educational opportunities if they do not have access to special preschool programs such as Head Start, which help them come closer to competing on an equal footing with their more affluent counterparts. Consistent efforts must be undertaken to help students appreciate cultural differences and view the United States as a stew, rather than a melting pot.

Multicultural instruction must be geared to the learning styles which culturally-different students bring to the classroom. Students who speak English as their second language must not be allowed to fail because of their language barriers. Obviously, this requires English as a Second Language (ESL) instruction, bilingual instruction when necessary, or preferably both.

Gender sensitivity relates to subtle factors such as using the masculine pronoun when referring to both genders. For example, writing in the plural rather than the singular, automatically necessitates the use of words such as "people" rather than "he" or "she." Also, attempts should be made to ensure that the curriculum guides and instructional materials are free of words or pictures which suggest racist or sexist stereotypes. All books, tests, and curriculum materials should be carefully evaluated in order to ensure that they are free of racist and sexist content.

Finally, it is critically important to ensure that strategies exist for including low-income and parents of color in the various school activities. Staffing patterns should reflect the racial/ethnic/gender balance that exists in a given community. Parents from diverse backgrounds should be used as guest speakers in order for the students to have visible role models to enhance their education and create better attitudes about the types of occupations which are attainable for them. Disciplinary procedures should be the same for all microcultural groups and all student clubs and activities should be open to everyone. School lunch menus and library holdings should reflect the cultural/racial/ethnic diversity that is the nation's greatest resource.

REFERENCES

Banks, James A. 1991. *Teaching strategies for ethnic studies*. Boston: Allyn & Bacon.

Banks, James A. 1993. Multicultural Education as an Academic Discipline. *Multicultural Education*. (Winter): pp. 8-11, 39.

Banks, James A., and Banks, Cherry A. McGee. 1995. *Handbook of research in multicultural education*. New York: MacMillan.

Banks, James A. and Lynch, James, eds. 1986. *Multicultural education in western societies*. London: Holt.

Boateng, Felix. 1990. Combating deculturalization of the African-American child in the public school system: A multicultural approach. In K. Lomotey, ed., *Going to school: The African-American experience,* pp. 73-84 Albany, New York: SUNY Press.

Gollnick, Donna M. and Chinn, Philip C. 1998. *Multicultural education in a pluralistic society*. Upper Saddle River, New Jersey: Prentice-Hall Inc.

Gorski, Paul, et al., eds. 1999. *The multicultural resource series, professional development guide for educators*. New York: National Education Association.

Grant, Carl. 1994. Challenging the myths about multicultural education. *Multicultural Education* (Winter): pp. 4-9.

Josephy, Alvin M. 1994. *Five hundred nations*. New York: Alfred Knopf.

Koerner, Brendan I. 2000. When is it okay to drop out of school? Now, say some fundamentalist Christians. *U.S. News & World Reports,* 12, June 2000.

Kozol, Jonathan. 1991. *Savage inequalities*. New York: Crown Publishers, Inc.

Kuppers, Gaby, ed. 1994. *Companeras: voices from the Latin American women's movement.* London: Latin American Bureau.

Lau v. Nichols, 414 U. S. 563 (1974).

Mitchell, Bruce and Salsbury, Robert. 2000. *Multicultural education in the United States: A guide to policies and programs in the 50 states*. Westport, Connecticut: Greenwood Press.

Mitchell, Bruce et al. 1996. *The dynamic classroom: A creative approach to planning and evaluation,* Dubuque, Iowa: Kendall/Hunt.

Ogbu, John. 1987. Variability in minority school performance: a problem in search of explanation. *Anthropology and Education Quarterly,* Volume 18, 312-334.

Ravitch, Diane. 1990. Multiculturalism: E pluribus plures. *The American Scholar* 59 (3), 337-354.

Rosenblum, Karen, et al., eds. 1996. *The meaning of difference: American construction of race, gender, sex and gender, social class orientation*. New York: McGraw-Hill.

Schuller, Gunther. 1999. *The swing era, the development of jazz, 1930-1945*. New York: Oxford University Press.

Sleeter, Christine E. 1999. *Making choices for multicultural education*. Upper Saddle River, New Jersey: Prentice-Hall.

Takaki, Ronald. 1993. *A different mirror: A history of multicultural America*. Boston: Back Bay Books.

6

American Education
and the Courts

Throughout the history of American education, legislation and court actions have had dramatic impacts on the nation's public schools' equality of educational opportunity issues. Indeed, some of the Supreme Court verdicts have split the country in half. Decisions such as *Brown v. Board of Education* (1954) have motivated massive social revolutions which have impacted the nation's schools in dramatic fashion. Indeed, the membership of the U.S. Supreme Court has acquired major political overtones which have resulted in presidential elections focusing on the future composition of that body and the manner in which the Constitution might be interpreted. It is estimated that President George W. Bush, who assumed office in 2001, may appoint up to four members of the highest court in the land. Thus, the political implications are quite obvious. This president could drastically alter the course of American history.

THE NATURE OF PUBLIC LAW IN AMERICA

Some historians have viewed American law as a tripartite function. At the top is the U.S. Constitution and its many amendments. No laws can be passed anywhere in the country which are not "constitutional"; that is they must be in compliance with the Constitution and its amendments. Throughout the nation's history many laws have been passed which are unconstitutional. They remain intact until they are challenged in the courts and have been found to either be acceptable or unacceptable by that body. Moreover, each state has its own Supreme Court which can also rule on the constitutionality of state laws. The U.S. Supreme Court can either accept, overturn, or decide not to hear state decisions which are appealed to the highest court in the land. The U.S. Supreme Court is the ultimate decision maker, but it is important to remember that it does not have its own police force. That means that it is not the responsibility of that body to see to it that its decisions are carried out in actual practice. That is the responsibility of the U.S. Department of Justice.

Since the Supreme Court members are nominated by the president and affirmed by the U.S. Senate, one can quickly conclude that the constitutional interpretations rendered by the court are highly politicized. Presidents are quick to appoint justices who subscribe to their political and constitutional philosophy. Thus, it becomes obvious that in making decisions about who to elect to the presidency, voters should think very carefully about future court appointments which will be made by the president elect. Many political analysts believe that American voters seem to give short shrift to the importance of potential presidential nominations to the highest court since the nation seems to be enamored with form over substance at the present time.

In the middle of the tripartite model is the U.S. Congress, consisting of the House of Representatives and the Senate. In order for Congress to pass federal laws, a bill must be passed by both the House and the Senate. It then must be signed into law by the president. If the president vetoes a bill, that veto can be overturned by a two-thirds majority vote.

The third portion of this tripartite model includes the various regulations issued by federal agencies which relate to the actions approved by the U.S. Congress. Obviously, these regulations must comply with the language of the actions which have been approved by Congress and signed into law by the president of the United States.

In addition to this national legal system are the legal systems of the 50 states. They are quite similar in nature to the federal model, consisting of state constitutions (which must comply with the U.S. Constitution), state statutes, and the various regulations of state agencies. The local legal system depends on the charters of local governments, local ordinances, and local regulations.

RACISM IN THE NATION'S LEGAL SYSTEM: A QUICK HISTORY

Unfortunately, like many other countries around the world, the United States has endured a history of racism, some of which has impacted the legal system, affecting the nation's public education system. A number of these issues have been touched upon in previous chapters, but several key legal activities have impacted the public schools in the United States. These events are merely examples of actions that have had their roots in racism, often affecting the nation's public schools.

Of course, racist practices extend back even before the advent of slavery. One of the more astonishing racist beliefs was the attitude of the English who believed that non-Christians were of an inferior quality and therefore unequal to the conquering hordes from England. This attitude helped sow the seeds of "manifest destiny," a concept that allowed the strong to take land from the weak, simply because it was there. This attitude set the stage for enormous land grabs from the original Native American residents who were unable to combat the superior power of the invading Europeans and set the stage for the Cherokee Trail of Tears, during the presidency of Andrew Jackson. During the early years of westward expansion, frequent conflicts occurred between the invading Europeans and the Native Americans. In order to terminate the conflicts, Jackson spurred the Congress into final approval of a treaty negotiated at New Echota, Georgia, which made it possible for the government to relocate the original residents against their will. As a result of this act, huge numbers of Native Americans were forcefully removed to parcels of land west of the Mississippi River. The Cherokee Trail of Tears occurred because of this racist episode. While this despicable episode resulted in forcing the original landholders to leave their territory, it was not the last. Another similar event occurred during World War II when President Roosevelt forced Japanese Americans to leave their lands and move to relocation centers.

Shortly after California was admitted to the Union, another piece of racist legislation was enacted in California and upheld by the state's Supreme Court. This statute prohibited the testimony of African Americans, mulattos, Chinese Americans and Native Americans in cases involving European Americans. Justice Hugh C. Murray somehow concluded that Chinese Americans in California were a variety of Native Americans. Obviously, this action precipitated new hostilities against members of these four minority groups. Like the New Echota, Georgia treaty, this legislation did not relate directly to public education but it tended to solidify the belief of many Americans that a free public education was only needed by European American children because children from other microcultures were of inferior status and therefore, it seemed unlikely that the new nation would benefit through the expenditure of public funds for their education.

Perhaps the most controversial piece of legislation relates to the contradictions in the First Amendment to the U.S. Constitution. While one part of this 1791 amendment stipulates that Congress shall make no law respecting an establishment of religion or prohibiting the free exercise thereof, part two stipulates that Congress shall make no law which abridges the freedom of speech or of the press. Obviously, the first part (known as the establishment clause) comes into conflict with the second part which allows citizens the right to free speech.

At this writing, an ongoing conflict relates to the issue of prayer in school. Since the spate of Supreme Court decisions ruling against the instigation of public school prayer by either federal, state, or public school officials, the religious right has been instrumental in exhorting people to initiate the Lord's Prayer in public gatherings. If such practices are spontaneous, it is perceived that they will pass constitutional muster. Ironically, in Matthew 6:5-6, Jesus argued that those who prayed in private would be rewarded and that only the hypocrites liked to pray aloud on street corners!

The last legal issue to be discussed at greater length later in this chapter is the famous *Brown v. Board of Education* Supreme Court decision of 1954. As previously stated, this verdict had great effects on schooling in America, particularly as it related to equality of educational opportunity and a myriad of other social issues related to the nation's nagging problems of racism and inequality.

THE CHEROKEE TRAIL OF TEARS

While the Cherokees had endured a history of conflict with other southeastern tribes such as the Choctaws and Creeks, the discovery of gold in their regions brought the Europeans in ever increasing numbers. President George Washington issued a proclamation urging citizens to apprehend a group of "lawless, wicked persons" who attacked a town in the Cherokee nation. Five hundred dollars were offered for each of the culprits who were apprehended and convicted. The proclamation was also signed by Thomas Jefferson.

Shortly after this episode a group of European American vigilantes raced through Philadelphia, shooting at Native Americans and European Americans alike. This militia group actually occupied the city, and only through the pleading of European Americans was the rest of the town spared from further confrontations.

Early in the 1800s, two German American Moravian missionaries became interested in establishing educational programs for the Cherokee children. They told Arcowee, an old Cherokee chief, that they would send English teachers to them but they also indicated that they were extremely interested in converting the Cherokees to Christianity. This was one of the first attempts on the part of European Americans to provide any kind of formal education to Cherokee children. The interest in Native American education coincided with President Washington's beliefs in the need for Native American children to become educated. He argued that it might take up to 50 years for Cherokees and other Native Americans to become "educated" to a degree that might make them knowledgeable enough to participate as "American" citizens who could vote intelligently and make responsible decisions.

These educational attempts coincided with the efforts of the American Board to open schools for African American students as well as children from the Cherokee nation. While these efforts were applaudable, it is important to note that at this time in history, very few efforts were being expended on the education of Native American children in other parts of the country. Since education was not a federal function, the education of Native Americans was often left up to private religious groups such as the Moravians. However, the Cherokee tribe has exhibited an interest in education throughout its history. It is important to remember that the Native American tribes had no written language until a syllabary was developed by Sequoyah, a Cherokee. But while the Cherokees were among the most cooperative Native Americans in acquiring a Eurocentric education, it is important to remember that they had a late start as far as worldwide literacy was concerned.

When considering unequal educational opportunities, it is quite clear that the Cherokees and other Native Americans would have a difficult time achieving on the same level as their European American counterparts. The lack of a written language meant that many competencies taken for granted by other children, were unknown to many Native American youngsters who entered school. And while the federal government tried to compensate for this inequity through Bureau of Indian Education (BIE) schools and many other ploys, the gap was wide and difficult to close.

RACIST LEGISLATION IN EARLY CALIFORNIA

As mentioned earlier in the chapter, a law was passed in California which prevented African Americans, mulattos, Chinese Americans and Native Americans from testifying in trials which involved European Americans. The message in this piece of legislation was quite clear. These four minority groups were deemed inferior to the newly arrived Europeans. Moreover, the action signaled something else. At that time in history, jobs were scarce and European American workers carried their spirit of manifest destiny to all parts of the West.

Consequently, the European American workers were sometimes forced to compete for minimal-skill jobs with the newly arrived Europeans. It has been said that employers of Chinese immigrants, such as Charlie Crocker of the Central Pacific Railroad were quite pleased with their work ethic and their qualities of patience, intelligence frugality, and docility. However, for those who competed with them for unskilled labor jobs, the fact that they could work as hard as European American men and were willing to accept lesser wages, made them an unacceptable commodity. The hostility from the European American majority caused major problems for them.

A racist miner's tax was levied on Chinese laborers but later the California Supreme Court declared an equally racist "police tax" against Chinese Americans over 18 who were not miners to be unconstitutional. Other racist practices against Chinese Americans included an action during the 1860s that excluded them, along with African Americans and Native Americans from public schools. These and other actions would pave the way for the educational inequalities which have existed throughout the nation's history, plaguing the United States to this very day.

Interestingly, a later Supreme Court decision related to a Chinese American student resulted in a requirement that public schools must create compensatory education programs in order to ensure that all students have access to equal education opportunities. The plaintiff, Lau, argued that his constitutional rights to an equal education had been violated because the instruction in San Francisco schools was provided in English and his primary language was Mandarin Chinese. The U.S. Supreme Court agreed and as a result, it was necessary for the schools to provide children for whom English was their second language with special programs to compensate for this deficiency.

Most school districts utilized ESL programs and bilingual education programs to correct this problem. Unfortunately, several states terminated the use of bilingual education efforts in recent years. These instructional strategies had been instituted to comply with the 1974 *Lau v. Nichols* decision. Students were instructed in their native language when necessary in order to ensure that they would understand the language of instruction. It's an instructional strategy used in many other countries besides this one. A fact not well publicized was that in most bilingual education programs, students also received instruction in English in order to achieve a competency level which would eventually end the need for instruction in the student's native language. Sadly, it is quite likely that the termination of bilingual education programs could create an even wider gap in achievement between English-proficient students and their ESL counterparts, thus exacerbating the problem of educational inequality.

It should be noted that these examples of racist legislation all occurred in California. But similar legislation took place throughout the rest of the nation as well. However, these examples serve to illustrate the historical racist attitudes which have permeated the nation's history. Perhaps more importantly, the examples serve to illustrate the growing feeling that European American children are entitled to a better education than the ever growing non-European population.

THE FIRST AMENDMENT'S EFFECT ON
PUBLIC EDUCATION

Perhaps no American has had a greater influence on the modern day arguments about church and state separation than James Madison. At the same time King James I saw fit to maintain the English theocracy by punishing citizens who defected from the Anglican religion, Jamestown settlers established the Church of England in their new Virginia colony. However, by the middle of the 18th century, the American colonies contained thriving sects of Presbyterians, Separatists, Quakers, and Puritans, among others.

However, it was the Presbyterians who created a phenomenon known as the Great Awakening. The concept was particularly active throughout the middle colonies and this Protestant sect was greatly in favor of the revolution against England. But it was James Madison who became the primary architect of the First Amendment to the U.S. Constitution.

Elected to the Revolutionary Convention in 1776, Madison served on a committee that was charged with the responsibility of drafting a declaration of rights for the new government. He was passionately concerned about the dangers of establishing a state religion and along with George Mason, the Virginia statesman, set the stage for creating a constitution which made it illegal to do so

Madison voted in favor of establishing the Episcopal Church as a buffer against his concern over the possible tyranny of the majority. Great arguments ensued during the following years until 1789 when Congressman Madison convinced his colleagues to consider amending the U.S. Constitution. Originally, the present language of the First Amendment was the third of 12 options. But his influence prevailed and the First Amendment was officially passed 1791. The First Amendment stipulated that, "Congress shall make no law respecting the establishment of religion, or prohibiting the free exercise thereof; or abridging the freedom of speech, or of the press; or the rights of the people to assemble, and to petition the Government for a redress of grievances."

From the time the First Amendment became part of the Constitution until the 1940s, only a small number of cases were brought to the U.S. Supreme Court.

However, all that would change with *Everson v. Board of Education* (1947). The *Everson* case ruled that reimbursing the parents of private school students for transportation to and from their religious schools was constitutional. Previously, a Louisiana case (*Cochran v. Louisiana Board of Education*, 1930), ruled that it was constitutional to supply textbooks to children in religious schools. Also, a 1925 case (*Pierce v. Society of Sisters*, 1925), held that while states could require school attendance, students could attend adequate private schools if they so chose.

The *Everson* case ushered in a number of first amendment cases pertaining to religious issues which would have enormous impact on the nation's public schools. Just one year later the Supreme Court ruled on an Illinois program which permitted religious instruction during school hours in public schools. Students were released for this participation while other students remained in their classes. The practice was ruled unconstitutional (*Illinois ex rel. McCollum v. Board of Education*, 1948). This was an extremely controversial ruling that angered many religious right parents.

The *Zorach v. Clauson* case (1952), ruled that it was constitutionally acceptable for students to leave school during school hours in order to be involved in religious instruction, the last major first Supreme Court decision involving the establishment clause for a decade.

Perhaps the most controversial Supreme Court case involving the issue of church and state separation occurred in 1962. Because of a New York state law, a local school district decided to use a prayer which had been composed by the New York State Board of Regents. That body even established a procedure for its use and children not wanting to participate were excused. The U. S. Supreme Court declared the practice to be unconstitutional (*Engel v. Vitale*, 1962). This decision was rendered by the famous "Warren Court," under the leadership of Chief Justice Earl Warren. As can be expected, the decision infuriated the religious right and was influential in motivating dissatisfaction with the public schools by a number of religious groups. However, it is important to remember that the decision did not outlaw individual prayer, only statutes authorizing formal prayer in the public schools.

Another important factor in relation to this 6-1 decision is that the case was decided while Earl Warren was the chief justice, having been appointed by President Dwight Eisenhower. After the death of Chief Justice Vincent in 1953, Eisenhower appointed Earl Warren to become the Chief Justice of the Supreme Court. He adapted a libertarian approach in his deliberations and along with Justices Black, Douglas and Brennan, instituted a revolution in their interpretation of the Bill of Rights. Warren was a skillful leader and considered to be the second greatest Chief Justice (next to John Marshall) in American history by constitutional scholars.

The famous *Lemon v. Kurtzman* case (1973) had the effect of establishing a constitutional procedure for ruling on further first amendment cases relating to the establishment clause. The "Lemon Test" stipulates that legislation or governmental action must not have a religious purpose; must not have the primary effect of either enhancing or inhibiting religion; and must not create "excessive entanglement" between church and state. As can be seen from the

Lemon v. Kurtzman case, it became clear that the "wall of separation" between church and state would become a guiding principle in future separation of church/state issues.

At the present time, given the more rightward lean to the court, the Lemon Test has been attacked by Justice Scalia who declared that, "As to the Court's invocation of the Lemon Test: Like some ghoul in a late-night horror movie that repeatedly sits up in its grave and shuffles abroad, after repeatedly being killed and buried, *Lemon* stalks our Establishment Clause jurisprudence once again, frightening the little children and school attorneys of Center Moriches Union Free School District." The quote continues, but it can be seen by this section that Scalia seems bent on "driving a stake" through the heart of the Lemon Test. But even though the Lemon Test was not used in the 1992 *Lee v. Weisman* case, Scalia has been unsuccessful in his attempts to totally eliminate its use.

It should be noted that with the Supreme Court's insistence on the separation of church and state in line with the First Amendment's establishment clause, the religious right has persistently argued that federal controls have denied students the right to pray in school. Obviously, the charge is false. Students are free to pray wherever and whenever they like. In fact, as previously stated in this chapter, Matthew 6:5-6 even describes praying aloud in public as a less than desirable action! Nonetheless, states such as Alabama and Texas have tried to initiate formal prayer in school, and even at some school-sponsored functions such as football games. So far, the Supreme Court has been quite consistent in declaring such practices to be unconstitutional.

These actions have been quite controversial, particularly in the so-called Bible Belt and other areas. The religious right has been so angered by these Supreme Court decisions that such influential members as Robert Thoburn has declared that: "I imagine that every Christian would agree that we need to remove the humanism from public schools. There is only one way to accomplish this: to abolish the public schools. We need to get the government out of the education business. According to the Bible, education is a parental responsibility. It is not the place of the government to be running a school system."

Religious right strategies for getting rid of the public school system have included ploys such as running for the school board, not to make the public schools "better" but to shut them down. Unfortunately, recent Republican presidents Ronald Reagan and George Bush have needed the religious right for their presidential campaigns. While they never advocated shutting down the public schools, a la some religious right factions, they have made speeches in favor of school prayer and "family values" as defined by various religious right groups.

These practices have done serious damage to the public schools in that they have lost some of their more affluent/high performing students to so-called "Christian" schools. These and other events have contributed to such factors as declining test scores which has made it appear that the private schools are "better."

As can be seen, the First Amendment has been responsible for many problems in the nation's public schools. While the establishment clause has legally limited the religious activities which can be carried on, the freedom of speech section has created a great contradiction in the minds of some people. One of the biggest problems facing the nation at the present time is a seeming fascination with "freedom" without limitations. This can be seen in the number of lawsuits, the arguments over the "freedom" to pray, the militia movements, and the list goes on. But, a mandatory ingredient of freedom is responsibility. Without it, freedom is useless and anarchy is a probable outcome. But Americans do not seem to be overly interested in the responsibility factor at the present time. Thus, the conflict rages.

SCHOOL DESEGREGATION: A BLESSING OR CURSE FOR SCHOOLS?

As discussed in Chapter Two, the famous *Brown v. Board of Education* case undoubtedly had a stronger impact on the country than any Supreme Court decision in the nation's history. In fact, virtually all serious social scientists have argued that the case caused a social revolution of unprecedented magnitude. No case that dynamic occurs without other cases leading up to it and *Brown* is no exception. Most of the other cases and events have had to do with slavery and the growing opposition to this abhorrent practice. But even more basic, was the country's historical need for cheap labor which motivated the practice of slavery in the southern states.

Among the early events leading up to *Brown*, were the Fugitive Slave Act of 1850 and the *Dred Scott* decision of 1857. The Fugitive Slave Act made it possible for the federal government to assist southern slave owners in apprehending runaways, while *Dred Scott* ruled that freed slaves were not really free when they could escape to the North. These two actions stirred up even more anti-slavery sentiment in the country and helped pave the way for the start of the Civil War.

In addition to the 1896 *Plessy v. Ferguson* case (discussed in chapter one), was the *Cumming v. Board of Education* case in which the U.S. Supreme Court upheld a state of Georgia law which allowed the closing of segregated schools for African-American students when finances rather than racism was the reason. Interestingly, John Harlan, the lone dissenter in *Plessy,* sided with the unanimous majority in *Cummings.*

Shortly later in 1903, the *Berea v. Kentucky* case stipulated that the *Plessy* decision also applied to the private sector. Berea College, a school for low-income college students, had an integrated student body and refused a state order to become segregated. The college complied, sort of. To this day, the institution has maintained its programs for low-income students and is well integrated.

Another school case, *Gong Lum v. Rice* (1928), resulted in a verdict stipulating that a Chinese American girl could be forced to attend a school for African American students since the other school was for "white" students only. This case also meant that even though *Plessy* applied to the segregation of railway cars, the ruling also pertained to educational issues. It also signaled the country that it was okay to segregate other students who were not European Americans.

A major breakthrough in the road to desegregated schools came in the 1938 *Missouri ex. rel. Gaines v. Canada* in which the plaintiff, Gaines, sued the state for refusing him admission to the University of Missouri law school which was segregated for "whites only." This was one of the early cases brought by the NAACP to challenge *Plessy* and the ruling was that the state's policy was unconstitutional since there were no separate facilities for African American students. Eventually, the state of Missouri chose to create a separate law school for African Americans, and their segregated facilities were maintained. Of course, all of this changed after *Brown*.

As discussed elsewhere in the book, the *Brown v. Board of Education* case caused enormous changes in the nation. Not only did it overturn the notion of the prevailing "separate but equal" mind set, but it caused social changes on a level that American history had not quite experienced before. For some, there was a feeling of "it's about time." But for others it was an attack on cherished values of segregation and a way of life which had had its roots in the inferiority of African Americans and an insidious desire to live their lives in a racially segregated fashion.

For this latter group, the verdict in *Brown* was viewed as being immoral and illegal, since it violated their freedom to live a segregated life. Of course, this was particularly true in the South which had a long history of de jure racial segregation and a deep conviction in the inferiority of African American people.

The first schools in the country to be affected by *Brown* were the southern schools in states which had de jure segregation. As mentioned earlier, the U.S. Supreme Court has no police force to enforce its verdicts. That task is left up to the U.S. Department of Justice of which at first had little interest in entering a battle which would become extremely confrontational. The public schools in the South at first tried to avoid making changes at all. The tragic situation at Little Rock High School and the University of Alabama served notice that the southern history of segregation would not go away easily.

One of the major attempts to combat court orders for school desegregation occurred in Prince Edward County, Virginia, in 1958. Faced with court orders to desegregate its schools, the county decided to terminate public school funding. However, taxation funds were provided for the operation of private schools for European American children! While the closure was ruled unconstitutional by both Virginia's Supreme Court and a three-judge federal court, a district judge set the date of 1965 as the year in which the state should desegregate its schools. However, this action was declared to be unconstitutional and a district judge ordered the state to admit African American students to its public schools starting with the next school year (September 1959). Yet the defiant state found still another loophole and instead of complying with the federal order, agreed to a local option provision and refused to appropriate funds for the operation of public schools.

Instead, taxation funds were provided for the operation of segregated schools for European American students. African Americans had no public schools open for a period of four years. The U.S. Supreme Court declared both actions to be unconstitutional. The logic was quite simple. The Fourteenth Amendment requires that the states provide an equal education for all children, regardless of race, gender, or ethnicity. The justices were also irritated that 10 years had elapsed since *Brown* and that the state had made a mockery of the "all deliberate speed" clause of this 1954 decision.

While a number of other similar practices occurred in the South, one factor which finally led to the racial integration of southern schools was college football. As the northern schools integrated their schools before the South, African American athletes matriculated in schools such as UCLA, University of South Carolina, Washington, Notre Dame, Michigan, Ohio State, and others. On the other hand, southern schools refused to accept African American athletes and as a result, their football teams had more and more difficulty in competing with integrated teams around the country. Although not well publicized, this factor motivated many southern universities to end their history of racial segregation and this helped public k-12 schools to do the same.

But the resistance to desegregation caused enormous difficulties for public schools in the South and later in the North. While the racism connected with de jure segregation was obvious, de facto segregation, a more subtle brand, occurred in the North. Since so many European American parents in both sections of the country rebelled at having their children attend school with African American students, those who were affluent enough simply took them out of public school and enrolled them in a variety of mostly segregated private schools. This resulted in another "brain drain," since research repeatedly has shown the positive correlation between per capita income and school performance. Obviously, whenever there is a large number of affluent students leaving the public schools, test scores and other performance levels show a decrease. Unfortunately, this phenomenon has contributed to the myth of private school superiority.

THE COURTS AND SPECIAL EDUCATION

One of the prime areas of world leadership which America's public schools do enjoy lies in the area of special education. The concept of a free and equal education for all has been around for many years now and the United States has attempted to provide educational services for all children regardless of their disabilities. The prevailing concept is that American children are entitled to a free appropriate public education.

While this attempt is applaudable, such practices simply can't occur in many nations around the world because of poverty problems. For example, developing countries such as Tanzania simply do not have the funds to engage in such enterprises, much as they would like to. But with this nation's red-hot economy it is possible to provide sophisticated programs for children with disabilities. However, it was not always that way.

As early as the middle of the 19th century, federal involvement in special education for disabled children became a role of the federal government through the establishment of special schools for children who were visually handicapped, hard of hearing, and mentally ill. However, it was not until World Wars I and II that other significant actions were taken for children with disabilities. Congress first authorized services for disabled veterans, and later expanded the concept to provide assistance for other persons with disabilities. Later, under the Social Security Act, benefits were made available to the visually handicapped, disabled, aged, and dependent persons.

During the Johnson administration in 1966, Congress created a new program for children with disabilities when it amended the Elementary and Secondary Education Act of 1965. Known as PL 89-750, this measure created a program offering federal grants to the states to assist them in initiating and expanding programs and projects for children with various disabilities. This 1966 legislation was repealed in 1970 when a new but similar program was established. However, by 1974, Congress was dissatisfied with the progress states were making and two key special education cases *(Pennsylvania Association for Retarded Children v. Pennsylvania* and *Mills v. D.C. Board of Education)* sent a message that children with disabilities *must* be able to receive an education in the public schools.

Prior to this time, some states had avoided their responsibilities in educating children with disabilities. But in 1975 Congress passed the Education for All Handicapped Children Act (PL 94-142) which required that children be educated in the "least restrictive environment." Also included in this act were the requirements that children be given nondiscriminatory evaluations, have zero rejections, and have an appropriate education.

The Individuals with Disabilities Education Act (IDEA) is the latest piece of major legislation affecting disabled children. Under this act, the state education agencies (SEAs) have responsibilities such as establish procedures for consulting with persons involved in the education of children with disabilities; give public notice for policy hearings; provide opportunities for public participation and comment; establishing procedures for making the state plan available to the public and parents; and to allow the general public to comment on proposed policies, programs, and procedures provided for in the IDEA before they are adopted.

Local education agencies (LEAs) must ensure that their applications for federal funds are available for review by anyone, particularly by parents of children with disabilities. IDEA requires that all records of children with disabilities are confidential and that parents and/or guardians have access to them. To ensure this confidentiality aspect, the Family Educational Rights and Privacy Act (FERPA) establishes the parameters of the various privacy considerations.

One of the most severe problems for public schools and LEAs has been the legality of providing services for private-school children. Historically, the public schools have been able to provide services for children with handicaps far more effectively than the private schools. However, a few private schools do specialize in special programs for children with disabilities. In some cases, individual educational program (IEP) deliberations have determined that a private school is the appropriate placement for a child with handicaps. Such a private school must be approved by the state. However, other children with disabilities have been placed in private schools by their parents. Often, the parents will discover that appropriate services are not available for their child in the private school. The question is whether such children are eligible for IDEA services.

According to the federal legislation, the local education agencies must " . . . provide special education and related services designed to meet the needs of private school children with disabilities residing in the jurisdiction of the agency." However, in general, the local education agency is not required to pay for the child's education at the private school unless appropriate educational programs are not available in the local public school. However, this concept is being challenged more and more in the courts and the issue often relates to interpretations of the First Amendment.

In general, if the courts find that the placement is not reasonable, the parents' costs can be reimbursed by the public schools. A 1993 Supreme Court Decision (*Florence County School District Four v. Carter*) related to the contention by parents that their child's IEP (judged to be adequate by the SEA and LEA) was unacceptable and the child was enrolled in a private school. The U. S. Supreme Court concurred with the appellate court's conclusion that the IEP was "wholly inadequate" and ordered the local school district to reimburse the parents for the private school costs.

Regarding the First Amendment issue, the Supreme Court ruled that the establishment clause of the First Amendment would not be violated by providing a sign language interpreter for a student enrolled in a private school after leaving the public school which was able to provide such an interpreter (*Zobrest v. Catalina Foothills School District, 1993*).

While it appears that these two cases have, in effect, tended to crack the wall of separation between church and state, there is also another message. In the case of students with disabilities, the IEP *must* be written in such a manner that the best educational interests of the student are protected. Further, for parents wishing to place their disabled children in private schools, it is necessary to ensure that the school has the special education services that are either comparable to or superior to those services that are available in the public school.

Nonetheless, these two cases illustrate a tendency to view first amendment cases pertaining to the education of children with disabilities in a different manner than cases pertaining to other church/state separation issues. The courts seem to be much more interested in examining the merits of the IEPs for children with disabilities compared to the concern over violating the establishment clause of the First Amendment.

In fact, it may be that a new attitude is emerging over the proper role of public schools. It seems that a number of people feel that they should be available for children with disabilities only when it's impossible for parents to find the required services in a private school. Perhaps the comments of a Southern California private school teacher in the authors' research survey summed it up best when she lamented the fact that her school was losing students because they no longer could send them to the public school for special education services. Obviously, she was referring to students whose IEP needs could only be met within a public school since her private school did not have adequate facilities.

On an encouraging note is the fact that both the courts and Congress have chosen to define the notion of educational equality in a very serious fashion when it comes to the issue of children with disabilities. Unfortunately, it seems that Congress and the courts have not yet chosen to include children from the culture of poverty as "children with disabilities."

VOUCHERS AND THE LAW: EFFECTS ON PUBLIC SCHOOLS

Throughout its history, the United States has invested a good deal of its resources in various reform efforts, particularly during the last half of the 20th century. After recuperating from the energy expended during World War II there was a relatively short period of tranquility. However, just nine years after the war ended, along came *Brown v. Board of Education* (1954), the Russian launching of Sputnik (1957), and the first Conant Report (1959), and a number of reform movements began in earnest.

A plethora of international comparisons of education efforts caused some to believe that the public schools in the United States were encountering some difficulties in maintaining their educational advantages over many other countries. While many of these concerns stemmed from the influx of non-English-speaking immigrants and an increasing proportion of students from poverty backgrounds, many critics of the public schools laid the blame on such factors as poor teacher preparation, a relaxation of educational standards, less than rigorous course work, and even not enough homework. Moreover, others laid the blame on a declining level of "family values" which would become a rallying cry for the religious right.

Early ideas for school reform included California's "Fisher Bill" which required all of the state's 6th-graders to have foreign language instruction. Interestingly, this unfunded mandate by the state legislature resulted in the creation of a television series called *La Lengua Lindo*, (The Pretty Language) , since Spanish was the most common foreign language spoken throughout the state. This program was viewed on television by 6th-grade classes.

In math, the instructional philosophy became based on the utilization of "set theory," an attempt to help children learn algebraic and arithmetic concepts in the elementary grades. It was an attempt to rearrange mathematical ideas which previously had been viewed as independent and discrete. The philosophy behind the changes was that this type of reorganization (referred to as "new math") would help students acquire a more in-depth understanding of the number system and the basic properties of mathematics.

In the state of Washington, a reform movement somehow known as "The Fourth Draft," attempted to do away with traditional ways of curriculum organization and evaluation, instead relying on the use of "performance criteria," a euphemism for behavioral objectives as developed by Benjamin Bloom, Ralph Tyler, and others. Interestingly, the chief architect of this particular reform movement was recruited by the state of Florida to carry out the same program in that locale.

At UCLA, Madeline Hunter developed her Theory into Practice models, insisting that the various pedagogical principles of her program must be adhered to religiously in order for students to achieve maximum educational benefits. The strategy became very popular, particularly in the state of Washington. A number of school districts in that state required their teachers to use Hunter's Instructional Theory into Practice (ITIP) approach. Some school districts refused to even hire teachers who were not well-grounded in this pedagogical practice. Interestingly, when the research results finally came in more than a decade after the program's inception, it was discovered that ITIP produced no better results than any other teaching strategies!

While these are but a small sample of the various reform movements which were vogue during the past 50 years, they provide an insight about the enormous unrest in connection with the nation's system of public education. Americans have always been interested in "quick fixes," and as is usually true with such undertakings, none of these seemed to solve the problems, both real and imagined, which plagued the public schools.

But to exacerbate the problem for America's public schools, during the Reagan Administration of the '80s, Secretary of Education William Bennett, argued that a crisis in America's public schools existed. He spoke of "failing public schools," and opined that industries were losing their competitive edge. He claimed that test results verified his highly politicized pronouncements. The American press reported his concerns as if they were totally true and consequently, the nation commenced believing that the American public school system was "failing." Bennett's prediction of industrial ineptitude proved to be incorrect, however, since the red-hot economy during the '90s was the greatest in the nation's history!

In fact, the aggregate test scores of high school seniors did decline between 1963 and 1975. However, what the press did not report, and what Bennett chose to ignore or was ignorant of was that during these years, new audiences of students from poverty backgrounds were taking the Scholastic Aptitude Tests (SATs). Moreover, using 1993 as a sample year, the percentages of students taking the SATs varied from under 10 percent in Alabama, Arkansas, Iowa, Kansas, Louisiana, Mississippi, North Dakota, Oklahoma, South Dakota, and Utah, to more than 70 percent in Connecticut, the District of Columbia, Massachusetts, New York, New Jersey, New Hampshire, and Rhode Island. Given the proliferation of educational research that reveals the significant statistical correlation between per capita income and test score results, it is really impossible to know what the scores even mean.

To further muddy the waters, the SAT was originally standardized to predict the success in college of high school seniors. In 1941, because of racial segregation and other factors, the students in the norming pool were from predominantly European-American students from middle income or affluent backgrounds. Thus, the original SAT score measures of central tendency were much higher than they were when more poverty children were in the testing pool.

To create a useful analogy, during the 1936 presidential election, the pollsters predicted that Alf Landon would become the next president of the United States. But, surprisingly, Franklin Roosevelt was re-elected in the biggest landslide in history! Unwittingly, the pollsters had sampled voters by telephone at a time in history when the country was suffering from the woes of the Great Depression and only affluent people could afford telephones! In other words, people who didn't have telephones went to the voting booth and opted for Franklin Roosevelt.

Just as sampling procedures are important for pollsters, so is the understanding of the socioeconomic structure of a testing pool if statisticians and/or politicians are to draw valid conclusions from test data. Such practices fall under the rubric of Research 101!

However, because of the misinterpretation of test results and the politicization of the whole process, public schools received a black eye which they probably didn't deserve. However, the public believed the rhetoric and unfortunately, during the same period of time that the arguments and concerns over "falling" test scores occurred something else was going on in the United States.

As previously mentioned, the growing number of Supreme Court decisions were angering adherents of religious positions which were to the right of center. The "wall of separation" between church and state was growing stronger, much to the dismay of religious right groups now headed by such prominent figures as Jerry Falwell and Pat Robertson. Due to their antagonism against the schools, they lobbied for attendance in private schools of their own religious persuasion. Moreover, the religious right literature actually argued against improving the public schools but instead opted for getting rid of them altogether and allowing parents to have access to vouchers which they could use on their children's education.

Since the courts had continuously ruled against their beliefs in the previously mentioned landmark Supreme Court decisions, their secondary strategy was to elect presidents who would appoint federal judges and Supreme Court justices who were amenable to the positions of the religious right. And since the Republican Party needed the religious right votes to win elections, the religious right soon became an important arm of the Republican Party. Thus, it can be seen that the entire set of issues involved became heavily politicized.

Two other strategies of the religious right were to elect their members to city councils, school boards, legislatures, and the U.S. Congress. In fact, during the year 2000 election, Pat Robertson promised that his Christian Coalition would help elect a "born again" president who would change the Supreme Court and try to end the concept of church and state separation. However, the other strategy of the religious right is to back a voucher system in the event that the public schools still remain intact.

THE SCHOOL VOUCHER FUROR

A common argument used by proponents of a voucher system is that as a "reform" strategy, voucher programs would force public schools to compete with the privates and improve in the process. Of course this argument is based on capitalistic notions of competition keeping prices low and producing better products. However, the temptation to equate the education of human beings with the production of goods is probably fallacious. Nonetheless, the interest in vouchers has been growing and has actually resulted in limited voucher programs in a few states such as Wisconsin.

Of course, the biggest argument against the initiation of voucher programs comes from the establishment clause of the First Amendment to the U.S. Constitution. Even so, were the issue to be decided in the U.S. Supreme Court at this time (September 2000), the verdict would undoubtedly be 5-4 and the direction could be anybody's guess.

The notion of providing vouchers to parents for placing their children in alternative schools is not a new concept. It is traceable to the '60s ideas of Milton Friedman and Christopher Jencks, a Harvard University faculty member who was then employed by the United States Office of Economic Opportunity. Several voucher attempts were defeated in Congress during the '80s.

Republican Presidents Ronald Reagan and George Bush, were proponents of vouchers and they campaigned for them in an attempt to make the concept more acceptable to skeptical Americans. This effort also failed, but by a much narrower margin. Other proponents of voucher programs have argued that such strategies would encourage more choice among schools, subject schools to competitive marketing principles, promote efficiency through competitive practices, improve the involvement of parents in the schools, help to achieve equal educational opportunities, and increase the number of private schools which would lead to better school performance. (Interestingly, based on the available data, this is highly unlikely because there is a limited supply of affluent students in the United States and research history has shown clearly that they score much higher on measures of educational attainment).

Opponents of voucher programs have been fearful that the creation of such educational enterprises would lead to the dismantling of the nation's public school system and could even result in the United States becoming a theocracy. At the present time, two states, California and Michigan have undergone campaigns promoting voucher aid to religious schools. In California, the effort was sponsored by Timothy Draper, a former member of California's Board of Education, and a Silicon Valley capitalist. He financed a costly effort to get his initiative on the ballot.

A right-wing Michigan millionaire, Dick DeVos, and the Roman Catholic Church hierarchy teamed up to get their own statewide voucher system on the November 2000 ballot. Both of these measures were defeated in the November 2000 elections. However, other efforts are on the drawing boards and so the battle between friends and foes of the First Amendment appear to be locked in a life and death struggle.

Examinations of national attitudes pertaining to the notion of having the government provide parents with tuition payments for non-public school attendance reveal conflicting results. In 1998, 51 percent of Americans favored this practice while 45 percent opposed it. However, just two years later, the annual Phi Delta Kappan/Gallup Poll study revealed that only 45 percent approved while 51 percent disapproved. In another question which asked if people favored or opposed allowing students and parents to choose private schools at public expense, just 39 percent approved while 56 percent opposed! When asked to rate the school attended by their oldest child, 70 percent of the parents gave their public school an "A" or "B." Just seven percent of the parents awarded their child's school a "D" or "F."

These statistics seem to verify what numerous other Kappan/Gallup studies have shown. Americans are satisfied with their local schools but it is the other ones they are suspicious of! Thus, it would appear that much of the negative concern over the state of public school education in America is invalid. In fact, it

would appear from countless interviews and observations that much of the movement from public to private schools is motivated by little more than an antagonism with the establishment clause of the First Amendment and the enormous
affluence affecting people during the '90s.

One of the problems of the right-wing arguments about voucher programs ben-
efiting the poor is that since affluent people are so insulated from poverty, they
rarely understand the enormous problems that the poverty powerless must contend with constantly. Rich parents are able to deal with transportation requirements, private lessons, special clothing, as well as the other costs connected with
private school involvement. Moreover, they usually have flexible time which
enables them to do volunteer work in the schools. Sadly, poor parents are totally
occupied with meeting survival needs. Providing food, clothing, and shelter for
the poor is a full-time battle which wealthy Americans never have to deal with.
Consequently, from this standpoint it is highly questionable that voucher programs
will truly help the poverty powerless who might opt for leaving their neighborhood public schools in favor of spending their vouchers in a private school.

Moreover, there is the problem of status which may exist when low-income
children commence attending private schools which are primarily the domain of
the affluent. Children often become quite cliquish and those who may not "fit in"
could encounter social problems which could hamper their educational lives.
However, insofar as equal educational opportunities are concerned, another issue
may make it even more difficult for low-income children to adapt to the environments of private schools which historically have been the domain of children
from more affluent families.

Studies conducted at the University of Southern California during the '60s
revealed that children from poverty backgrounds in the Los Angeles area had not
enjoyed the advantages of their more affluent counterparts. They had not been to
the ocean as often, nor had they visited such places as libraries, museums, etc.
This meant that that they had not had access to the same kinds of life experiences
of more wealthy children, Thus, it might be quite difficult for them to compete
successfully with more affluent children, not because of a lack of intelligence,
but due to a lack of life experiences which often translate into learning prowess.

This is not to suggest that under the right set of circumstances such children
might not eventually be able to compete on an even keel with rich children. That
was clearly demonstrated and by the famous teacher, Jaime Escalante, in the classic movie, *Stand and Deliver.* But it does mean that poor children who choose to
compete with more affluent youngsters might need to acquire certain out-of-
school experiences which would provide them with a better world view and hope-
fully would enable them to compete successfully with affluent children. Unfortunately, most private schools which would be receiving voucher support are not
geared up to provide such individualized services for poor children.

Unfortunately, many voucher programs probably would not be able to provide
appropriate financial assistance to children from poor families. Many of the proposed voucher schools around the country might be based on a "for profit" basis
which means that high-salaried CEOs with little knowledge about the intracies

of education might be making decisions affecting the lives of children. If they are "for profit," then attempts could be made to secure the cheapest labor possible. They could easily encounter the same problems which are so rampant in the country's failing Health Maintenance Organizations which are dispensing sometimes less than mediocre health care in order to turn a profit.

FOREIGN ATTEMPTS AT VOUCHER PROGRAMS

Another major concern comes from the disappointing results of some voucher programs in other nations. Research on Australia's voucher program (known as the Independent Schools Program) revealed that a five percent decrease in public school attendance occurred in the nation's public school population between 1976 and 1986. At the same time, enrollment in non-public schools doubled from 5 to 10 percent. Unfortunately, it was also found that the socioeconomic status of children became more polarized in communities in which both the public schools and independent schools co-existed. Sadly, the effectiveness of the public schools commenced to suffer. Moreover, the proportion of public school graduates from high school who entered college dropped substantially after the Australians established their Independent Schools Program. On the other hand, the proportion of independent school high school graduates entering college increased by five percent. Unfortunately, the same studies revealed that the general effectiveness of Australia's public schools commenced to decline.

France commenced providing federal support for private schools in 1960 as a result of the Deere Act. While advocates of voucher programs in the United States love to cite the French effort, there is one major difference in the two nation's educational systems. France is a fiercely egalitarian country and school funding is provided by the federal government which ensures equal funding levels throughout the country. Unfortunately, this is not the case in the United States where huge inequities exist in the funding of rich and poor school districts as well as rich and poor states.

Two major concerns have caused many Americans to be leery of voucher programs. First, they probably violate the establishment clause of the First Amendment and might do serious damage to the "wall of separation" between church and state, which was envisioned by Thomas Jefferson and James Madison. These strong feelings were reactions to the various theocracies which had created such major problems in Europe and helped conjure up negative reactions against any sort of private funding for public schools.

Other critics of public funding for private schools have argued that such efforts are further examples of "the rich getting richer and the poor getting poorer" since affluent private school parents would no longer have to pay tuition fees. The issue has also become heavily politicized, since most affluent private-school parents are Republicans.

The presidential and congressional elections of the year 2000 were bitter and acrimonious at best. Republicans were strongly in favor of vouchers while Democrats strongly opposed them. And of great importance to major legal issues affecting vouchers and other controversial issues, is the balance of the U.S. Supreme Court. Presently, this right-leaning body is headed by rightists Scalia, Thomas, and Chief Justice Rehnquist. They have vigorously fought the First Amendment concept of the "Wall of Separation."

How education will fare in the courts during the next four years is anybody's guess. The present Supreme Court will probably experience rather dramatic changes since at least two Justices will probably retire during the next four years. If this happens, there could be a number of new challenges to previous Supreme Court decisions pertaining to such matters as school prayer, funding voucher programs, school segregation, Bible reading in the schools, and many other similar issues.

REFERENCES

Abraham, Henry J. 1974. *Justices and presidents: A political history of appointments to the Supreme Court.* New York: Oxford University Press.

Alexander, Kern and Alexander, David M. 1995. *The law of schools, students, and teachers.* St. Paul: West Publishing Company.

Alley, Robert S. 1994. *School prayer: The court, the Congress, and the First Amendment.* Buffalo: Prometheus Books.

Anderson, Don S. 1999. The interaction of public and private school systems. *Australian Journal of Education,* 36, pp. 213-236.

Beck, Warren A. and Williams, Donald A. 1992. *California: A history of the golden state.* New York: Doubleday.

Benen, Steve. 2000. Voucher Doubleheader. *Church and state.* pp. 53-8. September.

Berliner, David C. and Biddle, Bruce J. 1995. *The manufactured crisis: myths, fraud, and the attack on America's public schools.* Reading, Massachusetts: Addison-Wesley.

Data Research, Inc. 1994. *Deskbook encyclopedia of school law.* Rosemont, Minnesota.

Ehle, John. 1988. *Trail of Tears: The rise and fall of the Cherokee nation.* New York: Doubleday.

Fischer, Louis et al. 1995. *Teachers and the law.* White Plains, New York: Longman.

Friedman, Milton. 1962. *Capitalism and freedom.* Chicago: University of Chicago Press.

Groves, Martha. 2000. School vouchers proposal dwarfs existing programs. *Los Angeles Times,* 7 September.

Johnson, Charles and Smith, Patricia. 1998. *Africans in America: America's journey through slavery.* New York: Harcourt Brace & Company.

Kimball, Charles A. 2000. No pray, no play trivializes piety. *Los Angeles Times,* 7 September.

McWilliams, Carey. 1999. *Factories in the field.* Boston: Little, Brown and Company.

Rippa, Alexander S. 1998. *Education in a free society: an American history.* New York: Longman.

Rose, Lowell C. and Gallup, Alec M. 2000. The 32nd annual Phi Delta Kappa/Gallup poll of the public's attitudes toward the public schools. *Phi Delta Kappan,* 82-1, (September) pp. 41-66.

Schrag, Peter. 1997. The near-myth of our flailing schools. *Atlantic,* October. pp. 72-80.

Thoburn, Robert. 1986. *The children trap,* Fort Worth: Dominion Press.

Turnbull Rutherford H. III and Turnbull, Ann P. 1998. *Free appropriate public education.* Denver: Love Publishing Company.

Ulmer, S. Sidney. 1971. Earl Warren and the Brown Decision. *Journal of Politics,* 33 (August), 690n.

Vose, Clement. 1959. *Caucasians only: the Supreme Court, the NAACP, and the restrictive covenant cases,* Berkeley: University of California Press.

Wasby, Stephen L., D'Amato, Anthony A. and Metrailer, Rosemary. 1997. *Desegregation from Brown to Alexander: an exploration of Supreme Court strategies.* Carbondale, Illinois: Southern Illinois University Press.

Zirkel, Perry A. and Richardson, Sherry Nalbone. 1988. *A digest of Supreme Court decisions affecting education.* Bloomington, Indiana: Phi Delta Kappa Educational Foundation.

7

If the Nation's Public School System Crumbles, So What?

Of course, this question is almost impossible to answer properly because of the difficulty in defining the word "crumble." For purposes of the discussion to follow, we have defined "crumble." as an overall condition which would lead to a public school system decidedly inferior to its present status. If it "crumbles" public education could be even more under-funded than it is at the present time. Unfortunately, this could result in a "brain drain" which could see the nation's brightest students continue to opt for various sorts of private school involvement while the public school system could conceivably became a "pauper school system."

While it is unlikely that such a scenario could actually take place, if some of the trends described in the earlier chapters were to continue, the nation's public schools could "crumble." or at least change into institutions which are much less effective than they have been throughout the country's history. But in order to begin this possible odyssey, we would like to discuss some problems which could possibly lead to the demise of the nation's public schools as we now know them.

MAJOR PROBLEMS FACING THE NATION'S PUBLIC SCHOOLS

We have argued up to now that presently, there seems to be a general conviction throughout the United States that public schools are substantially inferior in quality. It is almost as if the notion of "public" conjures up some strange image of automatic inferiority. Take the example of Oaks Christian in Westlake Village, California. Constructed with a golf course fortune, this brand new private high school has a student body of about 200 students who are there because of dissatisfaction with the public schools they have been attending.

Since the annual tuition costs $12,000, it is quite obvious that only students from affluent families are likely to attend. The school facilities include state-of-the-art sports facilities such as an Olympic-sized swimming pool, the latest computers, and even gourmet coffee! The student body comes from affluent areas such as Malibu, Pacific Palisades, the Conejo Valley, Simi Valley, and some of the most wealthy sections of the San Fernando Valley. Ironically, these public schools have already been noted for being among the nation's highest-scoring regions on statewide assessment tests.

There is one main reason that the students opt to attend this new school. That reason is its orientation as a nondenominational "Christian" school. The curriculum deals with Christian dogma and the teachers have to be "Christians." Students do not. Because of its private nature, students will study both evolution and "creationism." "Creationism" is an unconstitutional topic for public schools since its ideas are taken from the *Bible*. Because of the establishment clause of the First Amendment, its exclusion from the public school curriculum is one of the big reasons that so many students were ready to leave their own schools in search of a school curriculum which espoused such religious fundamentalist positions. Due to the affluent backgrounds from which the students come, it is almost a foregone conclusion that the test scores will be extraordinarily high, helping to expand the notion of "good" private schools versus their "bad" public school counterparts.

The issue of religion is an enormous one throughout the world and the United States is certainly no exception. And because of the First Amendment to the U.S. Constitution, public schools are unable to subscribe to religious positions. They must do nothing to promote any religion, nor should they do anything to discourage it. To complicate the issue, some parents have even left the public schools in order for their children to attend private schools which have a completely different religious orientation from their own. Such practices serve to underscore further the deep dissatisfaction that some Americans have with the public schools. Granted, these cases are rather insignificant statistically, but such examples do illustrate the attitude that many people seem to harbor at the present time.

Not surprisingly, a sizable portion of the parents whose children have left the public schools believe that they are entitled to vouchers which will defray some of their expenses for private school participation. Increasing numbers of voucher initiatives have occurred recently due to the unwillingness of state legislatures to tackle such volatile issues. Often, these initiatives are spearheaded by multimillionaires who are willing to fund voucher campaigns because they are convinced of the legitimacy of their cause.

HOME SCHOOLING

But, not all parents leave the public schools so their children can attend private schools. Some parents choose to home school their own children. These practices are carried out for religious reasons, dissatisfaction with curriculum content, quarrels with individual teachers or principals, the belief that their children aren't learning anything, racism, concerns for the safety of their children, elitism, and the list goes and on.

Since the education laws vary from state to state, there are 50 sets of legal requirements pertaining to home schooling. The legal parameters are established in the state legislatures and are usually enforced by the state Department of Education. Some famous educators, such as John Holt, have recommended that parents educate their own children at home and to facilitate the process he wrote a "how-to" book two decades ago. The book was quite uncomplimentary to the nation's "factory system" of public school education and Holt seemed to suggest that since the public schools are hopeless, home schooling is the only other viable alternative. He fails to even address the possibility that another option for disgruntled parents might be private schooling.

Moreover, he fails to discuss the plethora of legal requirements which exist from state to state nor does he seem to mention that in general, the nations' courts have the right to establish compulsory education laws. However, home schooling options are provided for in most states, even though they vary substantially insofar as their various stipulations are concerned. Cases such as *People v. Levisen* (1950) ruled that the state's compulsory attendance law only stipulated that all children should be educated, but the state could not determine that they had to be educated in a particular manner or in a specific place. Thus, it can be seen that the same rationale for allowing private participation seems to apply to home schooling.

Interestingly, a more recent Michigan case upheld a state law that required home-schooled students to be taught by parents who were certified teachers. In *People v. DeJonge* (1991) it was determined that the state's compelling interests outweighed the rights (in this case, religious freedom) claimed by the parents. Unfortunately, not all states have this requirement, which means that some parents may not possess the skills to instruct their own children.

Fortunately, it can be seen that while parents do have the right to home school their children, the common interest of the state concept makes it possible for states to enact certain requirements which prevent parents from having "carte blanche" rights to educate their children at home. Thus, the home-schooling requirements vary from state to state.

PARENT CHOICE

As the public schools search for ways to present their product in a more positive light, parent choice is an option which has appealed to many. Obviously, if parents have a choice of where to send their children they are more liable to be happy, more likely to be satisfied with the public schools, and more apt to support tax levies and bond measures. Of course, this is a far cry from the old traditional method of limiting children to their "neighborhood school."

But while the whole notion of school choice is a tempting idea, it is always necessary to examine similar practices in other countries. Even though New

Zealand is a country which is certainly not similar to the United States in terms of population, gross national product, extent of industrialization, racial/ethnic diversity, etc., it is considered to be an industrialized nation in which success in educational pursuits is closely correlated with socioeconomic status. These two factors do provide New Zealand with substantial similarities to the United States.

Unlike the United States, New Zealand's education system has been controlled through the nation's Ministry of Education, the standard procedure for most of the world. Beset with problems of poor-performing urban schools, the state embarked on a school choice program, relying on the same free-market principles which many school reform advocates argued would make the schools more competitive and consequently more successful.

In 1989, the controlling labor government abolished the country's centralized educational bureaucracy and replaced it with locally elected boards of education which were controlled by parents. In 1991, the new national government with its belief in free-market principles gave parents the right to choose which school their child would attend, giving schools with more applicants than they could accommodate the right to be selective in determining who they would accept. These reform efforts were known as Tomorrow's Schools. The central Ministry of Education continued to fund schools, draft national curriculum guidelines and operate an accountability system which relied on visitations from an independent Education Review Office.

Interestingly, New Zealand has no national standardized testing program so it has been difficult to obtain accurate measures of school performance as a result of the reform efforts. In spite of this lack, observers reported evidence of the popular reforms exhibiting an energizing effect on many primary and secondary schools in middle and upper-middle income areas. One such school, the Gladstone Primary School in Auckland, organized its school program around Howard Gardner's model of multiple intelligences. (Interestingly, nobody tackled J. P. Guilford's more sophisticated *Structure of the Intellect [SOI] model.)*

However, there was a negative side. Observers detected an increased level of polarization, particularly in registration patterns. Research showed that New Zealand parents of all races have judged the quality of the schools partly according to the racial and ethnic mix of the students in a given school. Schools with large numbers of European-New Zealander students were thought to be the "good schools." Those with large numbers of Maori and Pacific Islander students were thought to be inferior in quality. Obviously, this is similar to present conditions in the United States!

Studies conducted through the nation's Ministry of Education revealed that in Wellington, the proportion of Maori and Pacific Island students who ranked lowest in socioeconomic status jumped from 76 percent to 84 percent during a five-year period from 1991 to 1996. And the government-supported New Zealand Council for Educational Research also found that the reforms resulted in increased ethnic polarization.

As has been the case in other similar attempts, research revealed that the school choice reform efforts produced the usual winners and losers. The schools which were perceived to be "good" schools seemed to have little trouble in populating their schools with students from affluent families which historically produce high-performing students. Moreover, the more affluent New Zealand families tended to consist of European New Zealanders.

On the other hand, the undersubscribed schools tended to be populated with greater numbers of students who were difficult to teach. By the middle of the 1900s, New Zealanders spoke openly of downward spiraling schools with declining enrollments and teachers clamoring for transfers to the "better" schools. Market theory posits that similar to businesses, if schools are unable to compete successfully and attract students, they will close down and other schools will surface in order to provide a sufficient level of educational services. However, this didn't seem to materialize in New Zealand because of the reluctance of educational entrepreneurs to open schools when failure seemed imminent.

SCHOOL SAFETY

Another common reason for leaving the public schools relates to concerns about school safety. During recent years, the unfortunate events at Columbine High School in Colorado and similar shootings in Moses Lake, Washington, Springfield, Oregon, and elsewhere have caused many parents to move their children to private schools. While these shootings were extreme examples, school violence has indeed become a major problem for American schools.

While some of these extreme acts of violence have had to do with gang warfare which is often related to drug issues, other extreme actions have been carried out by children who are severely troubled. Some of them have been influenced by the growing number of web pages which exhort young children to join a variety of racist groups, many of which promote extremely violent practices. The increasing numbers of teenagers who are psychologically disturbed seems to be motivated by a combination of increased pressures for high performance, drug addiction, and the lack of psychological services available for young people, particularly those who are unfortunate enough to come from low-income circumstances.

It should be noted that in addition to these extreme acts of violence, the nation's schools have been attempting to deal with increased incidents of petty theft, extortion, and other acts of a criminal or quasi-criminal nature. Consequently, more and more parents are turning to either private schools or home schooling as an alternative to public schools, which are often perceived as "dangerous."

And while public schools are generally perceived to be more dangerous than their private counterparts, it is encouraging to note that in *Phi Delta Kappan*'s latest study on public attitudes about public schools, fighting/violence/gangs was listed "11 percent of the time as being the biggest problem facing public schools. This now ranks only ranks fourth compared to last year's ranking of second. Interestingly, 18 percent of Americans believe that "lack of financial support" is the major problem facing public schools. The percentage of people who believe this to be the biggest American problem in education has doubled in just one year!

Since the violence problems tend to be more severe in high poverty areas, it is not surprising that most urban school districts now have their own police forces, complete with patrol officers who are allowed to carry weapons in many instances. Obviously, these expenses detract from the funds that used to be expended on direct educational services.

ELITISM

Unfortunately, some parents choose to leave the public schools for elitist reasons. Obviously, this a very subtle issue and it is impossible to determine the extent of such practices. However, there is ample evidence that many parents have chosen to leave the public schools in order to "keep up with the Jones." As more and more American families have become wealthy during the past decade, there has been a greater tendency to find schools which have higher levels of socioeconomic status.

Never before in history has one country experienced the level of upward mobility that has occurred in the United States. This phenomenon has catapulted parents into new levels of economic wealth which has enabled them to shop for the very best of everything. So in addition to purchasing the most elegant clothes, homes, automobiles, and the like, so have parents shopped for affluent schools which are populated by high-performing students from wealthy backgrounds.

When more high socioeconomic schools were created during the robust economic era of the '90s, sociologists have been quick to point out that such practices have contributed to the resegregation of American schools. Much of this resegregation has occurred among the various socioeconomic levels. In spite of the economic advances experienced by people of color, European Americans are still more likely to become millionaires. As they acquire such positions and commence shopping for "good" private schools, they are more likely to have their children attend schools from the private sector which are often segregated in a de facto manner.

Harvard researchers discovered that when African American and Latino students are segregated into schools where the majority of the students are from other than European American backgrounds, it is very likely that these schools will have high levels of poverty. Sadly, concentrated poverty is almost always linked to poor schools.

Interestingly, this is not the case in segregated schools for European Americans. In these environments, the segregated students invariably come from middle income and/or wealthy families. Moreover, compensatory education programs, particularly those which fall under the Title I rubric, have had a difficult time making significant gains in the schools where the poverty concentration is high. This Harvard University research finding through The Civil Rights Project investigations would seem to question the wisdom of financially rewarding the schools which improve the most.

The 1954 *Brown v. Board of Education* Supreme Court decision declared that racially segregated schools were unconstitutional and should be desegregated "with all deliberate speed." However, this issue is so politically volatile that few educators, much less politicians, have seen fit to aggressively pursue legislative edicts which would once and for all put an end to racially segregated schools in the United States.

According to the previously quoted Harvard study, diversity in the classroom benefits students in numerous ways. In fact, when racially balanced schools in Louisville, Kentucky were investigated, 80 percent of the 1,164 students surveyed said that their integrated school experience helped them get along better with children from other racial groups. Also, 90 percent of the students said they were "comfortable" or "very comfortable" during discussions of controversial racial issues.

RACISM

Unfortunately, racism is still another reason for parents leaving the public schools. However, this reason is more subtle and much harder to identify. The chilling data from Morris Dees' Poverty Law Center in Montgomery Alabama, has pointed to the increasing number of white supremacist organizations throughout the land.

The increase in the number of resegregated schools occurred during the '90s which was the same decade in which the growing number of white supremacy groups also took place. And even though from a pure research standpoint positive correlations do not automatically indicate a cause and effect relationship, the increases in these two variables does cause wonder among serious proponents of multicultural education.

Many of these issues pertaining to racism and the damage it causes have been discussed earlier. But both authors are professors of multicultural education and both authors have heard people express amazement that courses in multicultural education are still necessary. And as discussed in their previous work, *Multicultural Education in the U.S.,* minimal efforts in multicultural education have existed in some states.

Obviously, racism is still a major problem in the United States, as it is throughout the world. The fact that the United States is a highly pluralistic society would seem to dictate that strong anti-racism programs should exist throughout the land. But sadly, at the present time, the main anti-racist efforts seem to be centered in hate crime legislation rather than in multicultural education efforts which are designed to help children acquire healthy, positive attitudes about American diversity before they acquire the deeply imbedded levels of racial hatred which can lead to incidents such as the recent Texas assassination in which an African-American man was murdered at the hands of three European-American Texans who committed the murder simply because the victim was an African American.

THE CHARTER SCHOOL FAD

Yet another attempt to provide parents with more alternatives has materialized through the development of charter schools. At this writing 36 states have legalized the creation of charter schools through legislative changes. These schools have been favored by many right-wing groups as well as the National Education Association (although with severe misgivings) and both George W. Bush and Al Gore. In some circles, charter schools are viewed as a "reform" effort.

Charter school students do bring the same "per student" amount on which the local school budgets are based. Thus, charter schools take away both students and funding from the normal public school setting. This sum can be as high as the $11,609 per student in White Plains, New York, or as little as $3,820 in Kansas. The curriculum and school standards are established in each individual school and they are not normally under the direction of the local school district.

Charter schools cannot teach religion since they must operate within the parameters of the U.S. Constitution because they rely on public funds. There is a huge variation in the themes addressed in the schools. For example, the themes range from an Afrocentric curriculum to performing arts and community service. Unfortunately, a lack of control groups prevents the generation of scholarly research endeavors. Thus, their results are usually based on non-scientific data collection efforts which tell the education community very little about their effectiveness.

While the charter schools are not open to commercial enterprise in most states, some entrepreneurial ventures such as Jersey City's Advantage get around this by finding local groups which will start a school "on paper" and turn its operation over to a company. Headquartered in Boston, Advantage utilizes a highly prescriptive approach called "Direct Instruction." Unfortunately, this procedure does not have a solid research background so little is known about its effectiveness. Advantage is headed by a CEO with no school teaching experience or experience as a school administrator. His company is in the charter school business primarily as a money-making venture.

Even though the public schools lose students, in addition to some funding through the inception of the charter school movement, many educators still fear that an extensive charter school movement will detract from the strength of the nation's public school system. However, at the present time about a half million students are involved in such enterprises and it appears that this alternative to the regular public school program will continue to grow. Many argue that this competition will lead to the improvement of public schools. However, whether intensive school competition will produce the same results as economic competition remains to be seen.

IF THE TREND CONTINUES, THEN WHAT?

At the present time, America seems to be at the crossroads regarding the future of its public schools. Indeed, in the presidential campaign during the summer and fall of the year 2000, both Al Gore and George W. Bush had a lot to say about needed "reforms" for the nation's public school systems. While Bush argued for school choice in the form of vouchers and also for more rigid testing, Gore rejected vouchers and opted for smaller classes and more highly trained teachers. Unfortunately, both candidates seemed to be reluctant in addressing key issues which could be more basic. Obviously, one issue has been the nation's reluctance to ensure that children from the culture of poverty have the same educational opportunities as those from wealthy families. Historically, this issue was not addressed seriously until President Lyndon Johnson's so-called War on Poverty. But while much was attempted and some progress was made, the nation's short attention span soon turned to other pressing issues.

And while the public test scores have been showing modest gains during recent years, the prevailing attitude still seems to be that the public schools are "bad" and the private schools are "good." In fact, many right-leaning politicians still habitually use the adjective "failing" when referring to public schools. One reason for referring to the public schools in that manner, may be due to the fact that as previously mentioned in this book, there seems to be a faction among the religious right which actually wants the public schools to fail so their private religious counterparts might prevail.

If this is true, then the next appointments to the U.S. Supreme Court will be crucial in determining the future of public schools in America. Some political scientists have argued that ultimately, the issue of spending public funds for private schools through voucher programs and other similar means, must be settled in the U.S. Supreme Court. If the court moves more to the right than it already is, it is highly likely that the religious right will prevail and public funding for private schools may become a nationally accepted practice.

CRITICAL FUNDING ISSUES

So, if school vouchers become legalized by the high court and private schools are publicly funded, the primary question will be where do the additional funds come from? Of course in the last presidential election, a major difference between the two candidates was how to spend a large budget surplus. George W. Bush lobbied for a large tax cut while Al Gore presented other options.

However, if history repeats itself, it is unlikely that large infusions of federal money will be available for financing public schools. Therefore, it is quite likely that only slight increases in funding will materialize, even if the economy remains robust. Moreover, it is highly possible that this funding level will vary greatly from state to state. For example, wealthy states such as California may do quite well, while the poorer states such as Mississippi and Arkansas may not.

But in the final analysis, it seems likely that while the funding for education may experience small gains if the economy remains healthy, America's public schools will probably not receive massive infusions of new money. Therefore, the states may be forced to make some hard choices regarding their education budgets. Obviously, if the U.S. Supreme Court upholds the practice of using public funds for private school vouchers, the public schools will have substantially less money with which to operate.

In the past, substandard funding has resulted in larger classes, poorer preparation of teachers, inferior teaching materials, inadequate supplies of textbooks. and necessary curriculum materials, substandard computers for student use, and immense cutbacks in such programs as library services, music and art, and other school services such as health care, custodial services, physical maintenance of school plants, and a myriad of other programs which historically have related to quality school programs.

If these cutbacks should occur in the midst of a major economic recession or a major economic depression similar to the "crash" of 1929, the public schools could fall on hard times which are difficult to envision at the present time when the American economy is healthier than ever before. Obviously, such a situation could be disastrous for a public school system which is legally responsible for providing equal education opportunities for all American school children. Moreover, it could result in the public schools in the United States becoming a pauper school system.

The worst case scenario could indeed result in a totally disastrous situation for the nation's public schools which have served the country so well throughout its history. Indeed, it must be remembered that through the first half of the 20th century, the United States public school system was viewed as a world leader. Educators such as John Dewey, Horace Mann, and John Goodlad were renown world leaders in education and the public schools reflected their ideas and leadership. For example, the nation's public schools led the world in the creation of such programs as gifted and talented education through the work of E. Paul Torrance, Joseph Renzulli, Mary Frasier, and many, many others.

It also must be remembered that the United States has been a world leader in such fields as physics, medicine, space exploration, the arts, and a myriad of other areas. Indeed, the number of Nobel Peace Prize awards reflects this leadership, and it has always been the public schools which have led the way. But in addition to these outstanding achievements, the public school system in America has always provided hope for children from the culture of poverty because they have been accessible and most importantly, they have been free.

Unfortunately, if public funds are siphoned off for the development and maintenance of private schools, many poverty children may not be able to attend such schools which can attract wealthy high-performing students for a variety of reasons. Not only is it easier for private schools to exclude students for economic reasons, but they do not have to accept all students, regardless of gender, race, ethnicity, or intellectual talent. If the private schools cannot meet the needs of children who have physical, mental, or emotional problems, or are from dysfunctional families, they can turn them away if they see fit to do so. Therefore, such children must attend public schools. And if their funding is substantially diminished because of vouchers for private schools, the facilities for meeting the needs of such children obviously will suffer.

This possible lack of funding could also have a devastating effect on teacher recruitment. An old adage goes like this: A parent asked her child what she wanted to do when she grew up. "I'd like to be a teacher," replied the child.

"But, wouldn't you rather be a lawyer or a doctor so you could make more money?" queried the parent.

"Well," responded the child. "If everyone became doctors or lawyers, who would there be left to teach the people who want to be doctors and lawyers?"

Obviously, the message in this conversation is clear. Teaching, indeed is a noble profession. But, if the profession is seriously under-funded, who will want to teach? In recent years, high school teachers in the Soviet Union were among the highest paid persons in that nation. In Japan, teachers have been viewed with reverence. Such is not the case in the United States. And if the funding for public education deteriorates because it is siphoned off to private schools, where will good teachers come from?

Another potential problem of underfunding public schools is perhaps the most terrifying. If the financing of public schools diminishes because of the need to provide public funds for private schools, how will that affect the issue of the "haves" versus the "have nots?" Obviously, if the public sees the quality of public schools slipping even further because of a lack of financial support, then even more people are likely to send their children to private schools. This could result in yet another example of the rich getting richer and the poor getting poorer. Of course, some people may well say, "So what? How can that affect me?"

Well, we have numerous instances throughout history of violent conflicts, revolutions, and other occurrences which took place between the "haves" and "have nots" due to economic isolation. Some social scientists have argued that as the distance between these two groups becomes too great, than more acts of violence such as takeovers or revolutions are more likely to occur. Since the nation has already suffered from a Civil War, it is not impossible to imagine the dire consequences of future civil conflicts which might occur between the rich and the poor. Of course, the schools are powerless to deal with such possibilities. Only political actions can deter the possibility of this growing gap becoming so severe that ugly civil conflicts could occur. And sadly, these political actions depend on the attitudes of the voting public as to the importance of maintaining a strong and viable public school system.

Another issue which is part of the public schools' survival equation relates to school safety. Elsewhere in the book, we have referred to the problems of increasing violence, particularly in the public schools. Public schools do not have the luxury of cavalierly dismissing students who are viewed as trouble makers or who are "uneducatable." They are charged with the responsibility of trying to provide educational programs for dysfunctional children, children possessing the previously mentioned problems, and children who hate school and all persons associated with such enterprises.

Private schools could have expelled students who exhibited the problems of the Columbine High School assassins who were obviously disturbed and in need of the counseling that they never received. Public schools are charged with the responsibility of providing a suitable education for students and others with deep emotional problems such as these.

Throughout the book we have also referred to problems of racism, one factor which has motivated many parents to withdraw their children from public schools in favor of attending their private counterparts which tend to be more racially homogeneous. This practice occurred shortly after the previously mentioned *Brown v. Board of Education* Supreme Court decision which made racially segregated schools unconstitutional. However, during the past two decades, an increasing number of parents have opted to withdraw their children from public schools because of a belief that schools with predominantly European-American students are superior because they have a dearth of children of color.

Sadly, racism, while addressed during the civil rights movement of the '60s, still exists, and the evidence is that it is increasing. Indeed, the number of "skin-head" organizations is on the increase around the country, along with anti-Semitic groups, such as the infamous Aryan Nations organization in Hayden Lake, Idaho. Fortunately, that enterprise is now bankrupt and at this writing, its founder, Richard Butler is trying to find a place to live since his compound must be sold in order to pay for the court-ordered legal settlement.

Unfortunately, these racist attitudes still constitute one of the reasons that people withdraw their children from public schools in order for their children to attend private schools which are populated with mostly European-American students.

Thus, if these trends continue, it is quite likely that the country might end up with a two-tiered system of education in the United States. The top tier would consist of affluent, mostly European-American students who attend private schools which might be populated with high-performing students from families with extremely high educational aspirations. On the other hand, the public schools could become populated with mostly children from low-income and/or dysfunctional families in under-funded schools with lower performing students who struggle in the public schools that have been viewed as failing institutions by the general public. The students could be quick to pick up these attitudes of inferiority and their school failure might easily become a self-fulfilling prophecy.

REFERENCES

Clark, Christine. 1998. The violence that creates school dropouts. *Multicultural Education* (Fall): pp. 19-22.

Fischer, Louis, Schimmel, David, and Kelly, Cynthia. 1999. *Teachers and the law*. White Plains, New York: Longman.

Fiske, Edward B. and Ladd, Helen F. 2000. *When schools compete: A cautionary tale*. New York: Brookings Institution Press.

Graham, Patricia Alberg. 1998. Paying Attention to our Children. *Current*, May: pp. 3-7.

Hinrichs, Fritz. 1996. Classical education. *Practical Homeschooling*. No. 14 (November, December).

Holt, John. 1981. *Teach your own*. New York: Delacorte.

Kohn, Alfie. 2000. *The case against standardized testing: Raising the scores, ruining the schools*. Westport, Connecticut: Heinemann.

Kolbert, Elizabeth. 2000. Unchartered territory. *The New Yorker*, October 9. pp. 34-41.

Mitchell, Bruce and Salsbury, Robert. 2000. *Multicultural education in the U.S.* Westport, Connecticut: Greenwood Publishing.

Orfield, Gary. 2000. *Civil rights project*. Cambridge: Harvard University.

Peabody, Zanto. 2000. Oaks: Private school to open its doors to new student body. *Los Angeles Times,* 28 August.

Rose, Lowell and Gallup, Alec M. 2000. The 32nd annual Phi Delta Kappa/Gallup poll of the public's attitudes toward the nation's public schools. *Phi Delta Kappan.* 82-1, pp. 42-64. September.

Waymack, Nancy L. and Drury, Darrell W. 1999. Class-size reduction and student achievement. *Policy Research Brief* (National School Boards Association) (Summer/Fall) pp. 1-4.

8

A Blueprint for Saving the Public Schools

As can be seen from the discussions in the previous chapters, America's public schools appear to be in a crisis mode. Threatened by decreased funding due to voucher programs; the negative image incurred because of constant attacks by right-wing politicians and inaccurate press releases; the ignorance of the public in general regarding the relationships between per-capita income and school performance; constant attempts by the religious right to attenuate the establishment clause of the First Amendment; the proliferation of standardized testing; and other factors too numerous to mention, the public schools presently seem to be on the verge of major collapse in some parts of the country.

This seems to be due partly to the very basic structure of the political/ governmental system itself. During the last election both George W. Bush and Al Gore expounded on their educational promises. Many of the promises cannot be met because the federal government has no control over the local level, a phenomenon we described in the first chapter of the book. But while education is not mentioned in the Constitution, U.S. Supreme Court decisions require equal educational opportunities, racially integregated schools and the separation of church and state. Unfortunately, neither presidential candidate seemed to expound on these issues during their year 2000 campaigns.

Of course, the basic issue that Americans must be willing to face is can the public schools be saved and if so, how? Obviously, this subject is highly controversial and heavily politicized. But if the ideas of Jefferson and others pertaining to the necessity of strong public schools are still of value, it appears that a number of things must happen. The authors believe strongly in the value of the nation's public schools. Consequently, we feel that they are not only worth saving but their demise could easily lead to a national catastrophe. Therefore, we would like to suggest some possible remedies which might help.

FUNDING PUBLIC EDUCATION IN THE UNITED STATES

This blueprint for survival starts with the funding of public schools. Various equalization formulas have been proposed around the country but the fact remains that money talks, and since 1980, the gap between the "haves" and "have nots" has been growing. Unfortunately, this phenomenon occurs in the schools and impacts the lives of public-school children from various socioeconomic backgrounds. The enormous advantages enjoyed by children from high-income circumstances are well known and have been discussed elsewhere in this work. A number of rather subtle practices occur throughout the land which provide a big edge to high-income children. An interesting case in point occurs in California at the Ventura County Maritime Museum. During recent years, many school children have visited the museum. In addition to the outstanding museum is the Channel Islands Marine Floating Laboratory which allows children to expand their understanding of life in the sea through first-hand observations of ocean animals and plant life on a small ship named the Coral Sea. Most of the participants have been affluent children from private schools due to the fees which are charged. Fortunately, a Title I grant has made it possible for students from low-income schools to participate in programs which previously unattainable due to the costs.

Thus, without special funding it can be seen that affluent children have opportunities such as this which can provide them with numerous educational benefits, giving them an incredible edge over their less affluent counterparts. Although the example cited may sound relatively insignificant, affluent children often have access to many other subtle advantages of this nature which may translate into enormous educational experiences which are not available to children from poverty homes.

Presently, funding for public schools comes from two primary sources: state appropriations and local levies. Obviously, this creates inequities between local school districts with lucrative tax bases and those which may not be able to levy the required funds so easily. Also, inequities exist between states. For example, southern states such as South Carolina and Mississippi have a more difficult time funding their schools than Connecticut and Michigan which have stronger industrial bases which translate into a higher funding potential for schools.

In addition to local and state funding, federal funds are available for special title programs such as the Elementary and Secondary Education Act, Title I, a school reform law. While such funding efforts from the federal level are commendable, federal equalization formulas should be developed in order to fund all LEAs equally. The formulas could be based on a per-capita income basis and distributed to school districts under a blanket arrangement which would ensure that the funding in all 50 states was designed to put all of them on an equal footing educationally. Such proposals were absent in the campaign rhetoric of both George W. Bush and Al Gore during the 2000 presidential campaign.

Unfortunately, this concept has been attacked by some groups which are opposed to America's public schools. The unsubstantiated but popular rhetoric is that "throwing money at the problem won't solve it; what we need is more testing, better teaching and stricter accountability." While that argument has beguiled many, particularly those from anti-tax positions, it is an argument which begs the question and does not seriously address the main problem of America's public education system which is poverty itself. But discussing poverty is an uncomfortable pastime for politicians for obvious reasons.

The disparities between well-funded and under-funded schools are well known and recent studies have shown that funding does make a difference. For example, Kozol has argued that if the New York City schools were funded as well as those in Long Island, one class of 36 4th-grade children would have received $200,000 more invested in their education. This money would have paid for two more teachers which could have cut the class size to 18 students each with an extra teacher and plenty of money for field trips and teaching materials.

It is obvious that cutting class size can lead to better classroom performance with more individual attention, increased tutoring opportunities, and more field trips. It's the formula that many affluent private schools have been using to lure students away from overcrowded public school classes. These extra funds must be made available to the public schools. But even with the extra funding, the performance of poverty-stricken students cannot be expected to improve substantially during short periods of time because of the other problems which have plagued poverty children during their early years.

These difficulties have been articulated elsewhere in the book and as children get older the problems of poverty have become quite deeply ingrained in the psyche of school children who come from such backgrounds. Proper funding and appropriate strategies do make a difference and the slow growth, which will occur with proper funding, can help children to overcome many of their earlier barriers to learning which poverty engenders. Thus, the need for financial equalization assistance from the federal government is of paramount importance and is available because of the huge fiscal surpluses which have been predicted. Amazingly, neither presidential candidate chose to address this issue during their campaigns for the presidency during the year 2000.

One of the world's richest people, Microsoft's Bill Gates, argued that even providing all students with access to the latest technology will not solve the major world problem which is poverty. He went on to say that what is needed are massive infusions of monies to shore up the poorest countries of the world. He even went on to suggest that perhaps American citizens should be taxed in order to improve the lot of the tens of millions of poverty persons who struggle for survival throughout their entire lifetimes. That pronouncement sends a clear message to this country as well as the remainder of the world. The United States cannot be a truly proud nation until it refuses to allow its own children to be ravaged by the devastation that abject poverty produces.

Of paramount importance is the authors' underlying hypothesis that America's public schools are not "failing." It has become fashionable for some writers to use the adjective "failing" as part of the public school title. However, it's what we have, it's important, it is far better than we hear, and we can improve it even more. With that preamble in mind, here are some suggestions for making the public schools an even more viable, dynamic enterprise and a critical foundation of the nation's future.

HOW TO IMPROVE THE POVERTY SCHOOLS

Assuming that sensible equalization formulas do provide needed funds for poverty-pocket schools, it is true that special procedures will be required for meeting the needs of American children who have been raised in poverty. One basic need for such youth is the assurance that they can go to a safe home with good food, clothing, shelter, and proper parenting. While it is important for family groups to stay together if at all possible, some children will need to be removed from less than satisfactory home situations. While this may sound drastic, the best interests of the children must be considered. Presently, some of this is carried out through the work of state social workers and guardians ad litem who investigate questionable home settings and make recommendations for suitable alternative placements for children who suffer from physical and psychological abuse due to poverty or other unacceptable home conditions.

Granted, this sounds drastic, but unless the children are involved in stable home living situations, the best efforts of the finest teachers may have only minimal effects on the children. To accomplish this, more funds must be expended on needed social services. Presently, social workers around the United States are seriously over-extended and embarrassingly underpaid. In the long run, salvaging poverty children is far less expensive than incarcerating them for their aberrant behaviors, which is the current popular practice in the United States. Solving this enormous problem will require re-educating the American public about the need for increased social services which can only be properly provided through different budgetary priorities along with increased levels of taxation.

This change will be extremely difficult because of the nation's steadfast rancor over any kinds of taxes. It's an unpopular crusade for politicians and so it will require pleas from the super-affluent Americans, such as Gates, in order for this basic attitude change to occur. However, if it doesn't happen, the prevailing negative attitude about social service spending just might be the final nail in America's coffin. But it must be remembered that no other western nation has neglected its low-income youth more than the United States has.

WHAT THE CURRICULUM SHOULD BE

The public school curriculum has changed drastically in recent years. Due to the enormous influences brought by the proliferation of testing programs, the curriculum has become dominated by reading/writing and math/science. Teachers and principals have been forced to deal with increasing pressures for acquiring high test scores in the face of the mounting criticisms against the nation's public schools. This has forced public school teachers to spend inordinate amounts of time teaching young children how to take multiple choice tests and preparing for the test items that they will be dealing with.

In addition to the poverty factors mentioned previously, the other problem of test score measurement reverts directly back to the statistical procedures used in analyzing test data. For example, Texas set their reading standards at the 25th percentile. Of no surprise to anyone who had at least a cursory understanding of testing statistics, 75 percent of Texas students passed the reading test the first year! On the other hand, Colorado's reading standards were set at the median (50th percentile) and the writing standards at the 70th percentile. Half of the students tested proficient in reading but only 30 percent did so in writing.

None of these would be of any surprise to beginning measurement students, but the public, the media, and politicians laid the blame on poor teaching and failing schools. All it proved was that the public, the media, and politicians get failing grades in *Tests and Measurement 101*! Nonetheless, this shared ignorance serves to do a serious disservice to public education and public school teachers alike.

Another major concern is that the test-taking preparation in math/science and reading/language arts has forced teachers to give short shrift to other equally important subjects. For example, physical education programs are not uniformly required for America's public school children in spite of growing evidence that a lack of physical fitness can lead to major health problems. Fine arts programs have often been slighted as well as the social sciences and foreign languages. In addition, other important educational topics such as creative thinking development, futurism, the environment, and multicultural education, have diminished or disappeared because the statewide tests do not address these issues. Simply put, the tests dictate the curriculum, the ultimate educational folly!

Another concern of many educators is that students are being subjected to so many high-pressure test-taking drills in reading/language arts and math/science, that some students are starting to hate reading, writing, and math. Indeed, some educators are concerned that children may even grow up to become adults who will not want to read for pleasure.

Vocational educational programs have been on the wane in recent years for several reasons. Many high school students have opted for attending community colleges, four-year institutions, and public and private universities. Many of them have been convinced that a college degree will yield a higher income level. Much of this change has been due to the incredible economy which existed during the Clinton presidency. Consequently, many vocational programs around the country have had difficulty attracting students.

However, there are some signs that this robust economic era may be on the verge of changing which could produce a need for more American workers with vocational skills. Thus, the public schools may be well served to resurrect their vocational programs.

Of utmost importance is the total education of American citizens. History has proven that the cultures which have attempted to provide the most comprehensive educations for its citizens have been the most successful. Thus, the public schools should attempt to ensure that the education of young students should be both diversified and comprehensive. This requires the creation of curriculum sequences, which includes not only the important math/science and reading/ language arts components, but social studies (including strong history and geography strands), music, art, foreign languages, physical education, and drama. Moreover, these topics should stress the use of futuristic problem-solving models as well as multicultural education efforts, sex education, drama, dance, and environmental studies. They should be individualized adequately in order to provide for the most able learner as well as students who struggle academically.

Some have argued that young children should be subjected only to the three r's. However, it is our contention that children are capable of understanding important concepts related to all of the above topics as long as they are discussed at the appropriate levels of understanding based on the children's ages. This means that even five-year-old kindergartners are capable of learning simple concepts in the above areas.

WHAT TEACHING STRATEGIES SHOULD THE PUBLIC SCHOOLS USE?

The issue of how teachers should teach is a topic that has been written about consistently in professional journals. While there seems to be no consensus as to a specific teaching style that should be subscribed to, a number of characteristics seem to be consistently referred to as necessary. Teachers need to be intelligent, well-read, knowledgeable of student learning styles, inquisitive, willing to individualize their instructional procedures, and genuinely interested in their students. In addition to these requirements, they must also be in love with their craft. This is the most important factor because of the rigors connected with the profession, and the stamina it requires.

In order for the nation's public school system to continue its success, such persons must be recruited and paid well. Another important factor to consider is the preparation process itself which will be discussed later. In the classroom, teachers must be able to assess the needs of individual students and create teaching strategies which will meet the needs of individuals. For example, some students are kinesthetic learners and will perform much better if they can actually "feel" their learning. Such youngsters will probably learn to spell better by tracing letters on rough surfaces, such as sandpaper, with their fingers. Verbal learners may learn to spell better by merely hearing a teacher tell them the letters of a word that the student writes down. Obviously, if all students are being taught by using the same strategy, some will succeed but others may struggle.

While different types of learners need appropriate teaching strategies, another facet of individualized instruction relates to the intellectual level of students. Unfortunately for teachers, a roomful of students will usually exhibit diverse levels of intellectual proficiency. In order to meet these individual differences it is necessary for successful public school teachers to create differentiated approaches which are geared to the appropriate level of need.

For example, in reading programs, many teachers have been using three reading groups in a given classroom. Typically, one group reads "below grade level," another reads "at grade level," while the third group reads "above grade level." While this approach comes closer to meeting individual differences than keeping children together when their differences are great, another effective approach is the utilization of self-selected reading approaches which enable all children to read at their own level. The teacher works individually with students but also works with ad hoc groups when the need arises.

One of the current debates in reading circles is the "whole language approach" (formerly referred to as "the language experience approach") versus the use of phonics. This argument has been a cantankerous one during the second half of the 20th century and is really a useless argument. Both strategies are important, and successful public school teachers must be well versed in both procedures. The same is true for the other disciplines. In order for public school teachers to succeed, they must have knowledge of many different instructional procedures. Moreover, they need to be inventive and willing to try new strategies when the techniques in use are not successful. This is what medical doctors do and teachers should emulate that behavior.

For teachers, what we have discussed is intelligence, knowledge of many different instructional strategies, flexibility, stamina, innovativeness, creative problem-solving abilities, and even though not previously mentioned, a sense of humor which can prove to be the most valuable trait of all. These are the basic ingredients which help to mold successful public school teachers.

However, in spite of the need for such skills and talents, something else must occur. Talented teachers must be given the opportunity to utilize their own abilities as they see fit. Recently, many of the reform programs have relied too much on canned programs which have often been adopted by well-meaning school districts in an attempt to improve schools. Many of them have overused stultifying workbooks, materials of questionable merit, and various strategies which have robbed excellent teachers of the capacity to use their skills and talents to create their own individualized classroom programs.

Because of the spate of reform efforts during the past decade, entrepreneurs have been quick to sell programs to school districts which have been under relentless pressure to improve the schools. These pressures have placed school administrators and school districts in vulnerable positions which have required them to utilize programs which are designed to make money for corporations which have turned to the production of educational "quick fixes" for financial profit. Oftentimes these programs have had virtually no research data to substantiate the magnanimous claims CEOs have used to market their products.

EFFECTIVE TEACHER EDUCATION PROGRAMS

The history of education in the United States has been discussed in chapter one. As could be seen from the accounts thereof, teacher education was almost nonexistent until the 1800s, and even then it often required a person to spend as little as six weeks in a Normal School teacher education program in order to become certified. However, World War II marked a time in American history where teacher education commenced to undergo significant changes, which required more education than any time before.

At the present time, teacher education has become far more more rigorous than the programs which existed in the middle of the century. During the 1950s, the standard practice was for teachers to acquire a degree in education which stressed a number of teaching methods classes and a quarter (usually ten weeks) of cadet teaching. However, after the mid-century criticisms of American education, a number of changes began to occur.

Gradually, the requirements for cadet teaching grew more stringent as an answer to mounting criticisms about "unprepared" new teachers who had inadequate intern experiences. Universities such as Central Michigan, which had one of the nation's finer teacher education programs, required cadet teachers to have a second quarter of student teaching in another location in order to work with students who came from racial and ethnic backgrounds that were completely different from the student teacher's. The logic for this practice grew out of an awareness that the United States was becoming increasingly pluralistic and thus, it was posited that student teachers needed the experiences of interacting with young students from a variety of racial and ethnic backgrounds.

One University of Central Michigan student teacher completed a second student-teaching assignment at site on the Colville Reservation in eastern Washington after working with young students who were from the same racial/cultural background as her own. Thus, by the time she became a certificated teacher, she had already experienced two totally different types of students who had different life experiences, different worldviews, and different learning styles.

This procedure is exemplary and if the public schools are to improve, teachers must acquire experiences such as these. The prevailing literature seems to show that most American teachers come from lower- to middle-class backgrounds and a high percentage of them are of European American backgrounds. To compound the problem, a large percentage of students in teacher education programs have tended to grow up in racially segregated communities, which have provided very limited opportunities for multicultural involvement. Thus, the need for such pre-service cadet teaching experiences is obvious.

Another major change in certification procedures centers around the need for teachers to have a more mature understanding of the various disciplines aside from teaching pedagogy. Sound teaching pedagogy is of critical importance, but so is the need for teachers to have strong backgrounds in the disciplines they are responsible for teaching. Thus, an emerging trend nationally is the so-called "Master's Plus" program which relies on the recruitment of students who have already completed their bachelor of arts degrees. Some have even taught on emergency teaching certificates in order to alleviate the teacher shortages. They take a supplementary program which includes classroom teaching experiences, graduate-level courses in teaching pedagogy and other important master's classes such as history of education, school law, and the like. By the time candidates finish, they have become well-schooled professionals who have completed their master's degrees, and consequently have acquired a high level of scholarship, talent and experience. These programs are proving to be highly successful and are responsible for the placement of high-performing teacher professionals in the nation's public schools.

Obviously, America's public schools will never be more successful than the professional educators who staff the nation's classrooms. Their preparation programs must be designed to ensure that successful teaching candidates become intellectually curious; understand the needs of highly diverse children regardless of race, ethnicity, gender, and affluence levels; become loyal and participating members of the profession; evolve into effective mediators of macro and micro cultures; acquire the skills to successfully motivate student learning; and become a viable and contributing member of the school faculty.

This also affects schools of education which have been increasingly staffed with faculty members who have expertise in k-12 education but little experience in solid research enterprises. This has tended to compromise some of the academic rigor and professional scholarship. While schools of education obviously need some faculty members who have mastered the practical k-12 classroom experiences, a balance of scholarly research-oriented Ph.D.s are also needed in order to create a workable, effective balance in schools of education and departments of teacher education.

OUTSTANDING PRINCIPALS NEEDED
FOR PUBLIC SCHOOL SURVIVAL

School principals set the tone for public school effectiveness. First and foremost, successful principals must have been highly successful classroom teachers. This is critical because a good principal must understand the many nuances of successful teaching. They must be able to relate to the problems which are experienced by all teachers, both good and bad. This talent is basic and should supersede all other considerations. But in addition to this kind of experience, they must be able to work with all kinds of people since professional practitioners have a variety of unique personalities and good principals find ways to get along well with many different types of teachers and parents.

But perhaps most important is that they must have tolerant personalities which allow them to be comfortable in working with successful teachers who employ many different teaching strategies. Administering schools is at least partly pragmatic and therefore principals must have flexible leadership styles allowing them to be comfortable in knowing that successful teachers may utilize a huge variety of different teaching modalities which could all be successful.

Successful principals do not spend a great deal of time in their offices. Very little learning occurs there and few important school functions take place in that environment! Thus, the successful principals spend most of their time where learning occurs and where students are located. The successful public school principal needs to be a teacher, an organizer, and a strong public relations person who can interact effectively with students, teachers, staff, and parents. And while all of these things are important, the good public school principal also knows what is going on in the school.

Good public school principals are also good judges of professional talent and they are constantly attempting to secure the very best teachers and staff members for their schools. This occurs through unobtrusive but consistent observations of the total school staff. If students and teachers are used to seeing the principals come into classrooms, the observation process becomes less obtrusive and consequently more successful. Frequent but short visits are generally much more successful than formal long ones.

Finally, good principals are not paternalistic. They believe in the competence of their teachers and staff and they choose not to interfere unless absolutely necessary. The first requirement of the good public school principal is to work with teachers to help them improve their skills and talents. When they are confident that they are fully functioning professionals, they encourage teachers to be responsible for their own classes and to make their own decisions. Moreover, they encourage their teachers to take active roles in helping to determine appropriate policies in the schools.

As can be seen from this brief summary, public school principals are critical cogs in determining the effectiveness of public schools. In order for public schools to improve, principals must insist that students and teachers perform as well as possible. The enthusiasm, leadership, and personality of the public school principal has a powerful effect on the success of the school. Dynamic leadership is a basic prerequisite for successful public school environments.

RECRUITING AND RETAINING HIGH QUALITY PUBLIC SCHOOL PROFESSIONALS

According to John Goodlad, positive change in public schools occurs because of good leadership which is provided over a long period of time. For public school principals, this means that their strong leadership influences should occur at the building level and that it is necessary for principals to have the longevity to become effective change agents. Unfortunately, one common practice is that good principals often are promoted to other jobs which pay more money. This may mean that a type of "brain drain" could occur among principals which could have an effect on schools.

Another problem for principals and teachers is the pressure for their students to perform well on the previously discussed standardized tests which are mandated by state legislatures and each state's Department of Education. Amazingly, there is some evidence that in some instances, performance expectations have been raised to unreasonable levels in order to make it appear that the public schools are failing! This contributes to the myth of failing public schools, thus increasing the public's perception that private schools are automatically "better."

As previously stated, public schools are as good as their teachers and students. Therefore, the question remains, how do you recruit and retain outstanding teachers? Good teachers have most of the same qualities possessed by school principals. They're dedicated, they care about children, and they're more interested in people-serving professions as opposed to careers which are primarily for making money.

Assuming that young teachers coming out of the college or university are bright, enthusiastic, and love their craft, the important question is, how do you keep them in the profession? The first answer which comes to mind is centered around their remuneration and their professional work conditions. Sadly, when people see such statements in print, they commence worrying about their taxes, becoming fearful that they might go up again.

But in order to retain the good ones, it is first necessary to recruit the best available candidates. Most school districts tend to wait until applicants come to apply for positions in the spring. A few school districts aggressively recruit new teaching candidates by going to universities and colleges with sound teacher-education programs and attempting to recruit the most outstanding candidates they can find. Some districts work with the university supervisors who help train cadet teachers.

Teaching is a profession which takes its toll on the total stamina of even outstanding teachers. Many change professions, explaining that they are simply "burned out." The question is how can you avoid that? One possible solution to the problem is through the employment of liberal sabbatical leave programs. Sabbatical leaves have long been viewed as important higher education programs, and indeed that is true. Sabbatical leaves have worked for college professors but they can work equally well for k-6th grade teachers who need a professional change of pace periodically. Sabbaticals give professional teachers the opportunity to conduct research, pursue graduate studies, or engage in a variety of activities that would enhance their teaching prowess.

A second way to retain good public school teachers is to lower the class size. While the research shows that smaller classes do not automatically produce better student performance, smaller classes definitely require less stamina for teachers. Moreover, smaller classes make it possible for teachers to individualize their instructional programs more effectively, which tends to improve both teacher and student morale.

Third is the matter of earning potential. If the earning potential is not there, the probability of losing outstanding public school teachers to other professions increases dramatically after eight to 10 years. Paying public school teachers well is necessary for another reason. Not too long ago, state colleges and universities really were free. For example, the student fees for one of the authors cost just $24 a semester when he was working on his teaching certificate. However, at the present time, public school teachers have often incurred many thousands of dollars in student loan obligations by the time they enter the profession. This adds pressure to the lives of young teachers who need to use all their energy in the performance of their professional duties.

Outstanding public school teachers need raises throughout their entire careers. Presently, even many of the top-paying states tend to have ceiling salaries that people reach after 10 or 15 years. However, most public school teachers have a 30- to 40-year career potential. This means that there is a strong possibility of almost no salary increases for teachers during a major portion of their professional career. These earning ceilings have caused the profession to lose many of its finest practitioners. Consequently, a maximum salary potential of at least $100,000 per year is not an unreasonable amount based on economic figures for the year 2001.

Finally, public school teachers need quality classroom aides. They should be paid paraprofessionals who have received the kind of training which would enable them to be the teacher's right arm. They would perform services that enhance the effectiveness of the teaching enterprise. Obviously, this would require a restructuring of the school finance strategies which are now in use around the country. It would require new funding by state legislators who have been reluctant to provide adequate funding for public schools in the past. Due to this reluctance and the economic inequality from state to state (discussed earlier in this chapter), some of these new monies should come from the federal government. But if the nation is really serious about providing the best education program in the world, it probably has to happen.

PUBLIC SCHOOLS AND THE FIRST AMENDMENT

The final part of this blueprint for preserving the public schools relates to the First Amendment to the U.S. Constitution. The First Amendment is written as follows: "Congress shall make no law respecting an establishment of a religion, or prohibiting the free exercise thereof; or abridging the freedom of speech or the press; or the right of the people peaceably to assemble, and to petition the Government for a redress of grievances."

During recent years, many cases have dealt with such issues as prayer before football games and other athletic contests, use of religious works such as the Bible in public school classrooms, and organized prayer in the schools. Up to now (2001), the U.S. Supreme Court has been rather consistent in ruling that organized prayer violates the establishment clause of the First Amendment. The concept relates to the notion that the state should not subscribe to any particular religion. However, it must not prohibit citizens from practicing any religion either.

As discussed earlier in the book, some groups have fought hard to insert various religious practices in the public schools. Religious holidays, such as Easter and Christmas, have become contentious issues and many lawsuits have related to these two holidays. However, as it now stands, the First Amendment is still the law of the land which means that teachers must not inflict their religious views upon their students.

This does *not* mean that teachers are prohibited from using such classic religions works as the Koran and the Bible in their teaching. In a pluralistic society such as the United States, the state simply must not attempt to promote a specific religion and the public schools must emulate this practice. Landmark Supreme Court decisions such as *Engel v. Vitale* and *Lemon v. Kurtzman* have sent powerful messages to public schools. The First Amendment has helped designate the

United States as one of the world communities which protects and tolerates religious freedoms. Thus, it is incumbent on the nation's public schools to continue championing the traditional concept of church and state separation.

REFERENCES

Berliner, David C. and Biddle, Bruce J. 1995. *The manufactured crisis: myths, fraud, and the attack on America's public schools*. Reading, Massachusetts: Addison-Wesley.

Fischer, Louis, Schimmel, David, and Kelly, Cynthia. 1995. *Teachers and the law*. White Plains, New York: Longman.

Glasser, William. 1992. *The quality school*. New York: Harper Collins.

Goodlad, John. 1984. *A place called school*. New York: McGraw-Hill.

Goodlad, John. 2001. Leadership for change. *Phi Delta Kappan,* 82:1, 200, pp. 82-85.

Kohn, Alfie. 2000. *The case against standardized testing*. Westport, Connecticut: Heinemann.

Kozol, Jonathan. 1991. *Savage inequalities*. New York: Crown Publishers Inc.

Scheer, Robert. 2000. Gates sends a message: a wired world can't end poverty. *Los Angeles Times,* 7 November.

Shepard, Lorrie. 2001. How to Fight a "Death Star." *NEA Today,* 19:4. (January) p. 19.

Starnes, Bobby Ann. 2000. On dark times, parallel universes and deja ju. *Phi Delta Kappan* (October) 82:2, pp. 108-114.

9

Epilogue

Originally, the central theme for this book was to be "Can elitism destroy the nation's public school system?" Then we decided to look at the notion of unequal education opportunity as being the most important issue facing public school education in America. Obviously, the two topics really go hand in hand. The public school "brain drain" that we commented on leads to unequal opportunities for children in numerous subtle ways. But on a happy note, after researching these two concepts and after interviewing dozens of people, we found that a huge majority of Americans do have a great deal of confidence in the nation's public schools and recognize them as being part of America's most important institution.

No question about it, the nation's public schools are under attack by the religious right and other right-wing groups. Critics such as Timothy Draper, a Silicon Valley entrepreneur and ex-member of the California Board of Education, has referred to the nation's public schools as being socialistic and in need of being privatized. He sponsored a voucher measure during the presidential election held in fall 2000. In Michigan, another multimillionaire launched a similar voucher effort in an attempt to weaken the public school system in that state. Fortunately for the public schools, both measures lost.

Obviously, utilizing public funds for financing private schools runs the risk of being constitutionally unacceptable because of the First Amendment. Both the California and Michigan voucher measures would have provided public funds for the financing of private schools, both secular and religious. The fact that both measures were rejected seems to be sending a message that the public is presently not ready to forsake the First Amendment principle of church and state separation.

Similar attempts are bound to be forthcoming. The public school attacks have become more frequent and with ever-increasing velocity. In considering such issues, it is important to remember that as previously discussed, people tend to like their local public schools. But it seems that they're a bit suspicious of the others!

Of further interest is the fact that attacking the public schools has almost become a favorite national pastime. The attacks come from all quarters: from corporate America to the religious right, to individuals such as Admiral Hyman Rickover, and Rudolph Flesch, who had their own educational axes to grind. The assault continues. As a matter of fact, the siege has occurred throughout most of the 20th century. In spite of it all, the nation's belief in the public schools has certainly not disappeared. In fact in the latest Gallup Poll on public education, 56 percent of public school parents awarded their local schools an "A" or "B." The same group graded the public schools nationally with an "A" or "B" just 22 percent of the time! The same poll also found that people viewed the Democratic Party as being more interested in improving public education in the United States while the Republican Party was deemed as more likely to support legislation which was more favorable to private schools. Thus, the "victory" of George W. Bush may not bode well for America's public schools.

The fact that Americans seem to be confident of their local public schools does not mean that public school educators can relax their vigil, nor should they. But those interested in keeping the public schools strong must be wary of political promises made by power-seeking candidates who will say anything about education that they believe will result in more votes. Meaningless catch phrases have been commonly used such as: "If I'm elected president, I'll strengthen public education by demanding higher national test standards"; "If I'm elected president, I'll make certain that every child's teacher has passed a stringent test which clearly demonstrates 'his' competency"; or "If I'm elected president I'll improve public education by putting 100,000 new teachers in the classrooms of America." The list goes on and on. However, the fact remains that the only people who can make such claims are state legislators, local school board members, and local educators. Promises from presidential and congressional candidates often have little meaning.

The pledges of presidential and senatorial candidates are critical from another standpoint, because they are the persons who are responsible for seating federal judges and U.S. Supreme Court members. Unfortunately, throughout history, American voters have exhibited alarming ignorance regarding the politicization of this process. What is clear is that the Supreme Court does have enormous clout in determining the future of American education in regard to the First, Tenth, and Fourteenth Amendments.

Perhaps the First Amendment is the most critical issue at the present time. Its establishment clause requires a "wall of separation" between church and state. However, many Americans from a plethora of religious right groups have pledged themselves to overturning the establishment clause of the First Amendment in order to allow religious activities to be carried out in the schools. Since many of these attempts will undoubtedly continue to be litigated in the U.S. Supreme Court, the political composition of that body may well determine the future of this volatile issue.

On a discouraging note for public school supporters, President George W. Bush has let it be known that his two favorite Supreme Court Justices are Antonin Scalia and Clarence Thomas, two of the nation's most far-right justices in history. Thus, if the new president is able to confirm new justices with similar political positions, the court could list even further to the right, putting the First Amendment in severe danger. Indeed, the nation could be in danger of becoming a theocracy.

Right-wing religious groups led by Jerry Falwell, Pat Robertson and others usually back political candidates from the Republican Party. They are countered by other organizations such as Barry Lynn's church and state group which seeks to keep the First Amendment's establishment clause intact and operational. This body and others like it usually support Democratic candidates. Thus, it can be seen that Supreme Court decisions affecting educational issues are heavily politicized.

The authors started the book by worrying that elitism might destroy the public education system in the United States. Then there's the other fear that educational inequality could become the Achilles tendon which could possibly lead to the demise of history's greatest public education system. Indeed, either of these issues could result in massive changes for the worst. But one of the most interesting outcomes in the year 2000 election was the resounding repudiation of Pat Buchanan who campaigned to get rid of the cabinet position for American education through the office of the secretary of education. The fact that Buchanan was clearly unsuccessful as a presidential candidate can probably be interpreted as a "thumbs up" for the federal interest in education. On the other hand, Buchanan's repudiation by the religious right clearly signals that group's loyal support for the Republican party. Their silence at the Republican convention clearly signaled that they had many markers which could be cashed in at a later time in return for their quiet but solid support of George W. Bush. Clearly, without this support, the Republicans could never have "won" the presidential election. The first marker to be cashed in resulted in Bush's appointment of John Ashcroft to the office of attorney general. Ashcroft, who lost his senatorial re-election bid to a deceased candidate, has been viewed as a hard-line member of the Republican right. This divisive appointment occurred just days after Bush's pledge to "bring the country together." With Ashcroft's confirmation, irreparable damage could be done to the nation's public schools through his rigid adherence to the Republican Party's negative attitudes about them.

Obviously, inequality in education intensifies when there are no national standards for education or any national financing. This places the nation's public schools clearly in the position of the "haves" versus the "have-nots." Children who are born in wealthy states or wealthy school districts will undoubtedly outperform poorer students. In a nation which has guaranteed "equal educational opportunity" for all students through decisions such as *Lau v. Nichols*, enormous disparities in educational opportunities, such as our earlier East St. Louis example, cannot be allowed to exist.

Having said that, we must also ask ourselves such moral questions as whether we should really be spending so much more on our military involvement than we do for education. Is that behavior justified? Indeed, the question is difficult because both enterprises obviously are required in order for this nation to continue its influence throughout the modern world. The question is who should make those decisions? Politicians who survive on soft money contributions from the influence peddlers for their re-election campaigns? Perhaps not.

But the United States is a highly diversified society and therein lies our strength.While this nation is certainly not free from racial, ethnic, and religious strife, diverse groups have been comparably cooperative and have managed to avoid the volatile and ugly ethnic cleansing wars of eastern Europe, the tribal conflicts of Africa, or the savage religious blood baths of the Middle East. However, this could change, particularly if the nation falls on difficult financial times and lower socioeconomic groups become pitted against each other in ugly trench warfare for economic survival.

Thus, the role of the nation's public schools becomes increasingly clear. Our schools simply must be serious about demanding equal educational opportunities without any regard for affluence level, religious background, race, gender, or ethnicity. Our nation's public schools must become serious about crafting viable and meaningful programs in multicultural education so that we can understand each other and defuse the mounting racism that is on the increase because of the new Web sites which promote racial hatred and Aryan supremacy. Our nation's schools must become reintegrated so that American school children can learn to value those who look different and yes, may even express themselves in different language patterns. History has continuously demonstrated that people who live in isolation from each other often learn to misunderstand and mistrust each other. We can't let that happen here.

We need strong democratic leadership from state superintendents and local school district superintendents. We must move away from the glorification of power to the utilization of the strengths, intelligence, and creative problem-solving talents of students, teachers, parents, and school personnel so that we can make better decisions about the curriculum, the issues, and the other factors that can continue to not only make Americans happy with their local schools but satisfied with the national public education system as well.

How do we get all of this done? We certainly don't profess to have all the answers. But we do have the words of one of America's most brilliant educators, professor John Dewey. We used these words in the Preface of our book and we'd like to close with them because in a democratic society, we simply can't afford to forget them. They go like this: "What the best and wisest parent wants for his own child, that must the community want for all its children. Any other idea for our schools is narrow and unlovely; acted upon, it destroys our democracy."

Selected Bibliography

Alexander, Kern and Alexander, David. 1995. *The law of schools, students, and teachers*. St. Paul: West Publishing Company.

Banks, James A., and Lynch, James, eds. 1986. *Multicultural education in Western societies*. London: Holt.

Backrach, Peter. 1967. *The theory of democratic elitism: a critique*. Boston: Little, Brown & Co.

Berliner, David C. and Biddle, Bruce J. 1995. *The manufactured crisis: Myths, fraud, and the attack on America's public schools*. Reading, MA: Addison-Wesley.

Binder, Frederick M. 1974. *The age of the common school*. New York: John Wiley & Sons.

Butts, R. Freeman and Cremin, Lawrence A. 1953. *A history of the American culture*. New York: Holt, Rinehart, and Winston.

Clark, Barbara. 1992. *Growing up gifted*. Columbus: Macmillan.

Conant, James. 1959. *The American high school today*. New York: McGraw-Hill.

Cremin, Lawrence A. 1982. *American education: the national experience*. New York: Harper and Row.

Dewey, John. 1916. *Democracy and education*. New York: Macmillan.

Glasser, William. 1992. *The quality school*. New York: Harper Collins.

Gordon, Edmund G. 1999. *Education and justice: A view from the back of the bus*. New York: Teachers College Press.

Guilford, J.P. 1967. *The nature of human intelligence*. New York: McGraw-Hill.

Howe, Kenneth R. 1997. *Understanding equal educational opportunity*. New York: Teachers College Press.

Kohn, Alfie. 2000. *The case against standardized testing: raising the scores, ruining the schools*. Westport, Connecticut: Heinemann.

Kozol, Jonathan. 1992. *Savage inequalities*. New York: Crown Publishers, Inc.

Mitchell, Bruce and Salsbury, Robert. 2000. *Multicultural education in the United States: A guide to policies and programs in the 50 states.* Westport, Connecticut: Greenwood Press.

Rippa, Alexander S. 1988. *Education in a free society: An American history.* New York: Longman.

Takaki, Ronald. 1993. *A different mirror: A history of multicultural America.* Boston: Back Bay Books.

Torrance, E. Paul. 1962. *Guiding creative talent.* Englewood Cliffs, New Jersey: Prentice-Hall Inc.

Turnbull Rutherford H. III and Turnbull, Ann P. 1998. *Free appropriate public education.* Denver: Love Publishing Company. 1998.

United States Department of Education. 1998. *State comparisons of education statistics: 1969-70 to 1996-97.* Washington, D.C.: United States Department of Education, National Center for Educational Statistics.

Zirkel, Perry A. and Richardson, Sharon Nalbone. 1988. *A digest of Supreme Court decisions affecting education.* Bloomington, Indiana: Phi Delta Kappa Educational Foundation.

Index

About the Authors

BRUCE M. MITCHELL is Professor Emeritus of Multicultural Education at Eastern Washington University. He is the co-author of *The Encyclopedia of Multicultural Education and Multicultural Education in the U.S.*, both available from Greenwood Press.

ROBERT E. SALSBURY is Professor Emeritus of Education at Eastern Washington University. He is the co-author of *The Encyclopedia of Multicultural Education and Multicultural Education in the U.S.*, both available from Greenwood Press.